EINSTEIN
&
NEWTON

Aaron B. Lerner

EINSTEIN
&
NEWTON

A Comparison of the Two Greatest Scientists

LERNER PUBLICATIONS COMPANY
MINNEAPOLIS

LIBRARY OF CONGRESS CATALOGING IN PUBLICATION DATA

Lerner, Aaron Bunsen.
  Einstein & Newton.

  SUMMARY: Explores and compares the life and works of
two physicists, regarded as geniuses, from childhood through
their professional careers.

  Bibliography: pp. 223-229

  1. Einstein, Albert, 1879-1955. 2. Newton, Sir Isaac, 1642-
1727. [1. Einstein, Albert, 1879-1955. 2. Newton, Sir Isaac,
1642-1727. 3. Physicists] I. Title.

QC16.E5L39 1973   509'.22 [B] [920]   72-7653
ISBN 0-8225-0752-8

International Standard Book Number: 0-8225-0752-8
Library of Congress Catalog Card Number: 72-7653

To PMES

Foreword

The Question of Genius

There is an eerie fascination about genius. It is so rare, so powerful, so unpredictable, so hard to understand. What is it that makes one human being tower so far above all the others? He seems no different in detail. He has eyes and ears as we do, senses and emotions. He has faults and virtues as we do, and in the faculties outside the realm of his genius, he may even be surprisingly diminutive.

How can we hope to inquire into this strange subject and end with something that ordinary human beings can understand?

Certainly, it would seem that in many fields genius is a law unto itself and cannot be restrained and confined by any limits drawn by words or logic. Who can define what it is about Picasso's lines or Wagner's notes or Shakespeare's words that make them so entirely and transcendentally different from other lines and notes and words?

After all, the difference in those cases lies in how the human emotions are affected. And who can define emotions, or even, in fact, be certain that emotions are affected at all. Perhaps it is only the emotions of a few critics that are moved.

In science, however, outstanding accomplishments can be measured. There we have guidelines that, ideally at least, do not depend upon the subjective reactions of human beings. The final test of genius in a scientist is how deeply and powerfully he peers into the laws governing the universe as decided, not by ourselves and our feelings, or by a few experts and their feelings, but by the universe itself.

A scientific theory, however beautiful and elegant, however overwhelming in majesty and proportion, is nothing until the observations gathered from the universe itself present a match;

and until, from the theory, further observations that are predicted are indeed obtained.

The universe is the judge.

And since that is so, it is perhaps in science that we can best salt the tail of the bird of genius; that we can most nearly close upon it and hold it up to the light and study its iridescent feathers.

Of the sciences, that which penetrates most deeply and lies most nearly at the foundation of all the rest is theoretical physics; and in theoretical physics, two names stand out above all the rest. They stand out so prominently, indeed, that they are the two, and the only two, that are household words even among those of the general public who know no science.

They are Albert Einstein and Isaac Newton. These two are separated by over two centuries of time, but each, in his own time, was revered by ordinary men as a transcendent genius and as a virtual demigod. Each was regarded equally highly by his scientific peers. And the reputation of each remained undiminished after death.

Concerning Einstein and Newton, there is no question and there can be none. They stand alone and all others follow.

Why? What was it about each and about both?

It is to these questions, through comparisons and contrasts, that Dr. Lerner addresses himself. He has explored their lives and their work and presented here a sensitive, carefully documented study of scientific accomplishment. Dr. Lerner's work represents a genuine contribution to our deeper understanding of the creative process.

Isaac Asimov

New York, New York
September, 1973

Contents

"You are a very clever boy, Einstein, an extremely clever boy, but you have one great fault: you never let yourself be told anything."

H. F. Weber
A physics teacher in college

"This Einstein will one day be a very great man."

Marcel Grossmann
A college classmate

"I have no particular talent—I am merely inquisitive."

Albert Einstein

"I seem to have been only like a boy playing on the seashore and diverting myself in now and then finding a smoother pebble or a prettier shell than ordinary while the great ocean of Truth lay all undiscovered before me."

"If I have seen further it is by standing on ye sholders of Giants."

Isacc Newton

Preface

More than a century and a half separated the lives of two mathematical physicists who became the outstanding scientists of their day and perhaps of all time. The names of other scientific giants, such as Galileo, Copernicus, and Pasteur, do not ring with the magic of Einstein and Newton. Some say that these two men were the most intelligent people who ever lived. Using only pencil and paper, they formulated laws of nature. Their deductions opened the door to understanding gravity, heat, sound, electricity, radio waves, and many other basic phenomena of the physical world. They displayed a capacity for abstract thought, combined with creativity, that was unique among men. Formulas they derived have enabled other scientists to make accurate predictions about the universe. Because of Newton's law of motion, scientists could conclude that rockets would work in outer space as well as on earth. Einstein's equations of 1917 made the development of the laser beam possible in 1960.

Newton and Einstein accomplished not merely one or two, but several major scientific feats in the course of their careers.

Comparisons between men of undisputed genius are always difficult. Can the achievements of Shakespeare be measured against those of Newton or the talent of Bach be compared to that of Einstein? Yet, a comparison may be meaningful when, as is the present case, the men excelled in the same field.

Although they shared some personal and intellectual characteristics, totally different life-styles emerged in their later years. Newton achieved great wealth, withdrew from active participation in creative science, and sought honors and recognition. Einstein had a modest income, required few material possessions, remained a working scientist to the end, and was unimpressed by the accolades he received.

Newton was a religious enthusiast who spent long hours examining the tenets of his faith; Einstein, who had little use for the dogma of organized religion, was, nevertheless, considered a deeply religious man by those who knew him.

In spite of the obvious differences between Newton and Einstein, I have always wondered if their great achievements were not, of necessity, based on important similarities in their personal traits and in their lives. At the funeral of Fritz Kreisler, the virtuoso violinist, his widow exclaimed, "If only he had practiced!" Maybe Kreisler would have been even better had he practiced more; yet we know that at some stage in his life he must have practiced for hours. Mozart, Schubert, and Beethoven composed almost without effort—but only after a period of complete dedication to music. No matter how great one's potential, the novice does not run a four-minute mile or swim the hundred-yard freestyle in less than 50 seconds. What sort of dedication early in life enabled Einstein and Newton to prepare for their future accomplishments?

A comparative analysis must be unfair to Newton in one

respect and to Einstein in another. Since Newton was born over 300 years ago, and Einstein less than 93, we have more reliable information about Einstein, some of which comes directly from him. He was never vague about his position on subjects of scientific or public interest. Yet the full implication and impact of his ideas must await the future. If this book had been written in 1959, only four years after Einstein's death, I could not have said that his work led to the development of the laser. Newton's work was done so long ago that its full meaning is known. To find out how much truth, if any, was in my hypothesis, I logged hours of interviews with Einstein's friends and relatives, in addition to scrutinizing Newton's writings and visiting his birthplace.

By adhering to specific points of comparison, I have kept the double biography brief and have made no attempt to present a definitive biography of each physicist. For readers who are not scientists, I hope this book will provide insight into some of the factors involved in scientific creativity. For my fellow scientists, glimpses of their own lives or of the lives of close colleagues are provided.

Aaron B. Lerner

Yale University
New Haven, Connecticut
September, 1973

Acknowledgments

So many people have helped with various aspects of putting this book together that I have made a conscious effort to confine acknowledgments of their contribution to as few words as my indebtedness would permit. Those who knew Einstein personally not only provided factual material—much of which was not published before—but through conversation gave me a clearer insight into his personality. My information about Newton is meager by comparison.

Maximum credit goes to my wife, Dr. Marguerite R. Lerner, and to Einstein's secretary, Miss Helen Dukas. Marguerite provided the stimulus for me to begin this project and aided in much of the writing. Miss Dukas worked closely with Einstein for almost three decades. In the last seven years, she and I exchanged more than 120 letters and held several discussions in person. Her assistance was essential in determining the accuracy of the information about Einstein. A tremendous body of literature on Einstein already exists, but so much of it is exaggerated or simply not true that constant checking of the facts is necessary.

An extensive correspondence with Mrs. Frieda Talmey Gallum provided information about her father, Dr. Max Talmey, and his brother, Dr. Bernard Talmey. From an interview and exchange of letters with Elsbeth and Marcel Grossmann, whose father and grandfather assisted Einstein in many ways, came the wonderful letter of 1908 printed on pages 97-98. Other letters exchanged between Einstein and Grossman will be compiled by Miss Dukas and Miss Grossman and published elsewhere. Correspondence and visits with Dr.

and Mrs. Rudolph Nissen, Dr. Guy K. Dean, Jr., Dr. Otto Nathan, Dr. Cornelius Lanczos, Dr. Rolf Ehrmann, and Dr. Hans Albert Einstein yielded valuable information on many aspects of Einstein's life.

Gina Zangger provided photographs and information about her father, Dr. Heinrich Zangger, and from Dr. Peter H. Plesch, I learned about his father, Dr. Janos Plesch. Information on Dr. Hans Mühsam came from his wife, Minna, his niece, Betty Newman, his sister, Charolette Landau-Mühsam, and her nephew, Dr. E. M. Joel. Additional material was provided by Thomas and Peter Bucky about their father, Dr. Gustav Bucky; by Erika Juliusburger about her father, Dr. Otto Juliusburger; and by Else Segall about her husband, Dr. Gabriel Segall. Photographs of Einstein in Israel were obtained from Dr. Nathan Rosen, Mr. Meyer W. Weisgal, and Ruth Greenman. Information about Dr. Marcel Grossmann came from Drs. Alvin E. Jaeggli and J. J. Burckhardt.

Dr. Albert J. Solnit served as consultant for psychiatric and personality interpretations and analyses used in the book. Dr. Fredrick C. Redlich rendered the translation of the 1908 Einstein to Grossmann letter. Additional help and support came from Drs. George Rosen, Martin J. Klein, Vernon W. Hughes, Franklin Hutchinson, Harold J. Morowitz, and Stanley Bauer. I am grateful to Helene Ujlaky for her help with translations, to Jill Landsberg, Helene Fineman, Karin Kelly, and Nell Putzel for editorial assistance, to Agnes D. Kelly for typing, and to the late Elsa Schmid for the black and white print of her magnificent color mosaic of Einstein.

The Reverend Victor S. Daws of the Colsterworth Rectory kindly took me through the church and showed me the register giving the time of Newton's baptism. He also guided my tour through Newton's house, Woolsthorpe Manor. I also wish to thank Dr. H. D. Anthony for correspondence regarding the date of birth of Newton's mother.

And to Harry, my brother and publisher, go special thanks for his continuous efforts on behalf of this project and for allowing me to have the final word on matters editorial. The responsibility for errors is mine.

To learn as much as possible about the role that Einstein's letter to President Roosevelt played in the development of the atomic bomb, I wrote letters to General Leslie R. Groves, Dr. Eugene P. Wigner and Dr. I. I. Rabi who were themselves involved in the Manhattan Project. Their replies are given in Appendix A.

PART I

DEVELOPMENT AND WORK

1

Childhood and School Days

Isaac

On Christmas day 1642, between one and two o'clock in the morning, Hannah Newton, who lived in the hamlet of Woolsthorpe, near Grantham, Lincolnshire, gave birth to her first child. She named the boy Isaac to honor his father, a farmer who had died two months earlier at the age of 36. We do not know the mother's age. The baby was premature, so small and frail that his mother said he could fit into a quart mug. For days she worried that he might not live. After several weeks, it was necessary to place a bolster around the infant's neck for support. But the child survived his premature start and, 84 years later, died in Kensington.

When Isaac was three years old, his mother married a minister, Barnabas Smith, who lived nearby. The child was left at home with his maternal grandmother and her son while his mother moved into her new husband's house a mile or two away. Later she bore three more children, the first being a daughter.

Isaac was his mother's favorite. Although they lived at least a mile apart, she treated him with affection and tenderness, as did the grandmother. The child was frail and usually played by himself. Gifted mechanically, he liked working with his hands and applied his skill to creating toys and gadgets. While other children played traditional games, Isaac tried to invent new ones. He made kites for himself and also for other children. He tended to be more friendly with girls than boys and built them little tables, cupboards, and other household equipment. He made bookshelves for his room and, from directions in a manual, constructed sundials, a water clock, and a windmill. With great care, he copied drawings of birds and mathematical figures. Remembering Newton as a child, a former playmate said, ". . . Isaac was always a sober, silent, thinking lad. . . ."

On weekdays Isaac walked to elementary school in nearby Skillington and Stoke. At 11 he attended King's School in Grantham, seven miles north of his home. Isaac generally kept to himself in school. He was quiet, serious, thoughtful, and somewhat suspicious. Competitive sports did not interest him. At King's School he ranked next to the bottom in the lowest form. Once an older boy punched him in the stomach. After classes, Isaac challenged the bully to a fight and beat him. Not only did he triumph over the boy physically, but he made up his mind to surpass him scholastically. Without much effort, Isaac rapidly rose to be the top student.

When Isaac was 14, his stepfather died, and two years later the boy left school to help his mother, stepbrother, and stepsisters run their farm. Although the family was financially comfortable, they needed his help with the farm chores. During the time at the farm he also began taking notes on projects of personal interest. His notes included such odds and ends as career possibilities, linguistics and phonetics, geometrical problems, and recipes for homemade medicines and chemicals.

While at King's School, Isaac had the good fortune to meet three people who were to help shape his future: the Clark brothers and Henry Stokes. Most important was the apothecary, Ralf Clark. Isaac lived with his family during the six years in Grantham. He read Clark's books and helped him in his work. The apothecary's brother, a physician educated at Cambridge, was the mathematics teacher at King's School. Dr. Clark taught Isaac mathematics and probably was responsible for his going to Cambridge later. The intellectual stimulation and guidance Isaac received from the Clark brothers as he developed from the ages of 11 to 19 undoubtedly were significant.

Henry Stokes, Headmaster of King's School, recognized Isaac's talents. After Isaac left school at 16 to help his family on the farm, Mr. Stokes repeatedly asked Isaac's mother to let the boy finish at King's School and go on to college. The teacher was determined. He said that he would forfeit his yearly fee of 40 shillings. After two years, Isaac's mother yielded to Stokes's pressure. At the time of Isaac's graduation, the Headmaster put him in front of the class and, with tears in his eyes, talked about the young student's outstanding intellectual and personal qualities.

At home or at school, Isaac was always a doer—he carved with his knife, worked with hand tools, or read books. An unusual ability to concentrate was revealed at an early age, as several stories illustrate. One day, on his way home from Grantham, Isaac was compelled to walk his horse up a steep hill. Thinking about some problem, he forgot to mount the horse

after climbing the hill and walked the animal all the way home
—a distance of five to seven miles. Sometimes while herding
the sheep, Isaac read or daydreamed. Often he forgot about
the sheep, and they wandered away from the farm. Nothing
suggested that he would be a good farmer. One evening during
a severe storm, the family worried about the animals and the
barn. But Isaac was not interested in that part of the problem;
he was trying to find a way to measure the speed of the wind.

At 19, shortly before Newton entered Trinity College in
Cambridge, he became engaged to Miss Storey, Ralf Clark's
stepdaughter. But they did not marry.

Albert

Albert Einstein was born in Germany on March 14, 1879, a
century and a half after Newton died. His birthplace was the
Bavarian town of Ulm, 85 miles from Munich. He died in
Princeton, New Jersey in 1955 at the age of 76. Albert's mother
was 21 and his father 32 at the time of his birth. A sister, Maja,
was born two years later.

As a son and first child, Albert was a much-wanted baby. His
mother and father were affectionate with him and with each
other. Friends described the parents as being "always on a
honeymoon." The father, Hermann, was a happy, optimistic
man and was not ridden by goals. Together with his brother
Jakob, Hermann Einstein ran a series of electrochemical fac-
tories, but they were unsuccessful. Hermann handled the com-
mercial aspects of their business ventures and Jakob, the technical side. The mother, Pauline, an accomplished pianist and
more ambitious than the father, read the classics to Albert and
initiated his study of music. When Albert was four or five and

recovering from a cold, his father gave him a compass. The boy, enchanted to find that the needle always pointed in one direction, played with the compass for weeks. He persistently questioned how it worked and remained deeply impressed. Albert could also sit by the hour and watch an ant colony at work. Much of the time he daydreamed and thought.

At about six or seven, Albert began studying the violin. After two years, the lessons were stopped, but he continued to teach himself. By the time he reached his teens, he had become a good violinist. He also taught himself to play the piano. Music became an inner necessity for him.

Until he was nine years old, Einstein did not speak fluently. Everything he said was expressed only after thorough consideration. He kept to himself. The maid referred to him as *Pater Langweil* (Father Bore), and his classmates called him *Biedermeier* ("square"). He had no interest in competitive sports and was not good at making things with his hands. He liked gadgets, especially finding out how they worked.

Two brothers, Max and Bernard, with an unusual but appropriate last name, Talmud, had a profound effect on Albert's education. Albert's father was a member of a synagogue in Munich. There he met Bernard Talmud, who had come from Lithuania to study medicine. The two became good friends. The Einstein family made a point of inviting a Jewish college student with little money to the house for dinner once a week. When Albert was between eight and ten, the guest was Bernard Talmud. During Albert's tenth to fifteenth years, Bernard's younger brother, Max, was the visitor. Both Max and Bernard were medical students with broad interests. Their father, Solomon, was a dedicated scholar of the Talmud, the basic book of Jewish law. Ordinarily the Hebrew word, *talmud*, meaning instruction or study, is not used as a personal name. In fact Max and Bernard changed their name to Talmey when they immigrated to the United States after graduating from medical school. Bernard became a psychiatrist and Max a specialist in diseases of the eye, ear, nose, and throat.

By the time Albert entered the Gymnasium, he had already learned the elementary principles of algebra from his uncle Jakob, a trained engineer. How much Bernard Talmey played or worked with Albert is not known. But Max found a boy whose interest in science was just awakening. The responsibility and opportunity to nourish the boy and guide his early course could not have fallen on better shoulders. Max had wide ranging interests. His love of learning was limitless, and he excelled in the art of self-instruction. Max described Albert as the "pretty, dark-haired, brown-eyed boy" with "exceptional intelligence which enabled him to discuss with a college graduate subjects far above the comprehension of children of his age."

Because Albert seemed interested in science, Max gave him a popular book on physics. Soon he brought a second book, then another. The two discussed each book before going on to a new one. When Albert was 11, Max gave him a textbook on geometry. Albert read it by himself and worked the problems. Each week Max checked the results and helped him with the more difficult problems. On his own, Albert proved that for a right triangle, the square of the longest side is equal to the sum of the squares of the other two sides. The 11-year-old stayed with this classic problem for three weeks. Max directed Albert's progression from geometry to higher mathematics. At 12 Albert began teaching himself calculus. Soon the boy was ahead of his teacher, and they switched to philosophy. At 13 Albert read Kant's *Critique of Pure Reason*, as well as works by other philosophers, and Max, as his teacher, knew that he understood them.

During the entire five years of their association, Max never saw Albert with boys his own age, nor did he see him reading light literature, not even a novel. Albert remained aloof and absorbed in books on mathematics, physics, and philosophy. Music was his recreation.

At the same time, Albert did not do well at school. His work was superior in science and mathematics but just passing in other subjects. His Latin teacher told him, "Einstein, you will never amount to anything," while Max Talmey said, "A *great* scientist or philosopher might be expected to develop out of that remarkable boy." To his school teachers Albert was an average student. To his teacher at home, he sparkled. Max thought he had discovered a child prodigy. Albert hated the rigidity of the Prussian educational system and refused to conform. To him, the teachers in the elementary school were sergeants, and those in secondary school were lieutenants.

At 15, with two years to finish at the Gymnasium, Albert was left in Munich while his parents, sister, and uncle moved to Milan. Within half a year, the boy's dislike of school intensified, and his loneliness grew so great that he decided to leave. He obtained a letter from the family's physician indicating his nervous state. On their own, some school officials had been trying to find a way to drop Albert because they thought he had a poor effect on student morale. A satisfactory compromise was reached. Albert received a certificate for completing mathematics and physics and a statement that he was doing passing work in all his other subjects.

Albert lived a wonderful half-year in Italy, enjoying his family and the cultural advantages of Milan. In the fall, at the age of 16, he left for Switzerland to take the entrance tests at the

Zurich Federal Institute of Technology. The examinations were necessary because, by leaving school early, he had not earned a secondary school certificate. He failed in modern languages, zoology and botany—subjects he had not completed at the Gymnasium. However, he performed brilliantly in the mathematics and physics tests and was asked to complete his secondary school education at the Cantonal School in Aarau, Switzerland and to enter college a year later. One sometimes hears that Albert failed his college entrance examinations in math. This is not true. In mathematics he was years ahead of his classmates.

To Albert's surprise, the Swiss School in Aarau was pleasant. He had freedom but still preferred to be a loner. One of his classmates pictured him well:

> As a young man he could not be fitted into any pattern. The atmosphere of the school suited the impudent Bavarian whose original nobility already distinguished him from all the others. Sure of himself, his grey felt hat pushed back on his thick, black hair, he strode energetically up and down in the rapid, I might almost say, crazy, tempo of a restless spirit which carries a whole world in itself. Nothing escaped the sharp gaze of his large, bright, brown eyes. Whoever approached him immediately came under the spell of his superior personality. A sarcastic curl of his rather full mouth with the protruding lower lip did not encourage Philistines to fraternize with him. Unhampered by convention, his attitude toward the world was that of a laughing philosopher and his witty mockery pitilessly lashed any conceit or pose. In conversation he always had something to give. His well-schooled taste acquired from traveling gave him a maturity of judgment. He made no bones about voicing his personal opinions whether they offended or not. This courageous love of truth gave his whole personality a certain cachet which in the long run was bound to impress even his opponent. . . . When he played his violin, the room seemed to broaden out. What fire there was in his playing! I no longer recognized him.

After the year in Aarau, Albert returned to Zurich and entered the Federal Institute of Technology at the age of 17. His parents had no funds, but money from two maternal uncles enabled him to continue his education.

Comparison

Einstein and Newton lived 237 years apart; yet as boys they shared striking similarities. To be sure there were differences. Isaac's father died before the child's birth. Emotionally, the young boy suffered even more when his mother left him in the care of his grandmother. His manual dexterity was exceptional. He had little exposure to music. Albert, on the other hand, was brought up in a secure family environment. He did not engage in handicrafts. Music was an intrinsic part of his life.

The boys' similarities stand out—some obvious, others subtle. Both were first born children. Each was followed by a sister. They were fathered by men in their early thirties. The mothers—and for Isaac after the age of three, the mother figure represented by his grandmother—were affectionate toward their sons and protective as well. Newton had no father, and Einstein's father was not threatening either physically or emotionally. No member of either family had been distinguished intellectually, professionally, or financially. Both children got off to a slow start. Isaac was premature and frail. Albert was late in talking. The youths, quiet and independent, kept to themselves and loved solitude. Neither played with boys his own age, and both avoided competitive sports. Each grew up in a family that left him largely on his own. They were not exposed to numerous brothers or sisters. The hallmark of genius —the ability to teach oneself—was evident early. Both boys were unusually inquisitive. They read much and often were seen with book in hand. A great ability to concentrate existed throughout their lives.

Although the parents could not provide intellectual help or stimulus, superb guidance arose from outside the family. For Isaac, it was the Clark brothers and Henry Stokes; for Albert, the Talmey brothers and Uncle Jakob. These men recognized the genius in their charge, and all responded in full measure. Had Stokes, and presumably the Clarks, failed to convince Isaac's mother that the boy should return to school after two years' absence and then go on to college, England would not have had Newton as its greatest scientist. Albert treaded equally precarious ground. If Uncle Jakob and Max Talmey had not encouraged Albert's intellectual development to soar when the boy's formal schooling was totally demoralizing, the world might not have had its Einstein.

Isaac and Albert were recognized as prodigies by the age of 12. Fortunately, they met no general acclaim. The conventional view that the boys could not be considered child prodigies because they did not perform unusual mental gymnastics at the age of five or six is incorrect. Isaac's spectacular talents were clear to his teachers in secondary school and Albert's to his personal teacher at home. Each boy undoubtedly benefited from not having his genius widely known at an early age. Their unique traits were allowed to develop without excessive intervention from the outside.

2

Unusual College Students

Newton

On June 5, 1661, Newton entered Trinity College at the University of Cambridge as Subsizer, working at menial jobs as college students do today. In January 1665, shortly after his 22nd birthday, he received his BA degree. Before graduation, he, along with 44 others, was elected a Scholar of Trinity College. Newton planned to continue his college career, but in June 1665, the University closed because of an outbreak of bubonic plague. He returned to his home on the farm in Woolsthorpe for two years.

As an undergraduate, Newton read Kepler's *On Optics*, Descartes' work in geometry, and Wallis' papers on mathematics. He was fortunate in being able to study geometry and optics under Isaac Barrow, an excellent teacher and the first professor to recognize Newton's superior abilities. Newton obtained a thorough knowledge of Latin, and also learned Greek, and some Hebrew, but no French or German. It was rumored that Newton did not do well in examinations. He worked hard but not for grades.

The one outstanding feature of Newton's college career was that he acted like a *graduate* student, not an undergraduate. He knew how to work independently. He gained no academic honors in his scheduled courses. His extracurricular achievements, however, included development of the binomial theorem and his first ideas on the calculus. He initiated observations on the refraction of light. In his last year at college, while studying intensely the path of a comet, Newton suffered the first of two nervous collapses. When he became involved with a project, he eliminated sleep and worked around the clock. But after the emotional breakdown, he forced himself to get some sleep every evening.

Little is known about Newton's personal habits, and it is difficult to separate fact from fiction. His social activities were limited. In his expense book he noted several visits to a tavern, and twice he recorded money lost at cards.

By the time Newton earned his BA degree, he and Miss Storey had broken their engagement. She married someone else, but the two remained good friends all their lives.

Einstein

During his four years at the Federal Polytechnical School from 1896 to 1900, Einstein's life in Zurich was simple enough. His meager monthly allowance gave him little leeway. He rented a small room from a family and, since he had no strong interest in food, was content with what he could afford to buy.

The pattern of self-learning begun as a small boy intensified. He had the superb mathematicians Hermann Minkowski and Adolf Hurwitz as teachers. Yet Einstein repeatedly skipped class—not to avoid learning but to learn more. Much of the time he was on his own, examining the works of Helmholtz, Hertz, Kirchhoff, and others. He de-emphasized exams, neither worrying about them nor cramming for them. Fortunately, Einstein's bright classmate, Marcel Grossmann, kept excellent notes and insisted that they study together before the tests. The opportunity to use good notes was fortunate because Einstein hated preparing for examinations and said, "It is a grave mistake to think that the enjoyment of seeing and searching can be promoted by means of coercion and a sense of duty... for examinations one has to stuff oneself with all this rubbish whether one wants to or not." Yet Einstein did well in college. His final grades, out of a possible 6 points for each subject, were 5 for theoretical physics, applied physics, and astronomy, and 5.5 in theory of functions.

The professors' opinions about Einstein varied. One thought he would not do well in physics and suggested that he study something else. Another considered Einstein bright but unteachable, while a third liked the boy's original solutions to many problems. It is fair to say that not one teacher in college recognized Einstein's genius. His fellow students were more astute and thought he was different and superior.

Einstein had four classmates, three boys and a girl. He and the girl, Mileva Maric, fell in love and were married shortly after graduation. All the boys earned PhD degrees, and one of them, Marcel Grossmann, became one of Einstein's closest friends. After meeting Einstein at 17, Grossmann told his own parents, "This Einstein will one day be a very great man."

Grossmann's loyalty was complete. When Einstein was graduated from college and did not have a job, Grossmann's father helped him get a position at the patent office. Einstein's PhD thesis was dedicated, not to his wife or first son, but "to my friend Dr. Marcel Grossmann." Grossmann later helped Einstein develop the general theory of relativity.

When Grossmann died in 1936, Einstein wrote to his widow:

> I remember our student days. He, the irreproachable student, I myself, unorderly and a dreamer. He, on good terms with the teachers and understanding everything, I a pariah, discontent and little loved. But we were good friends. . . . Then the end of our studies—I was suddenly abandoned by everyone, standing at a loss on the threshold of life. But he stood by me and thanks to him and his father I obtained a post in the patent office. It was a kind of salvation and without it, although I probably should not have died, I should have been intellectually damaged. And then, ten years later, our feverish work together on the formulation of general relativity. We were and remained friends throughout our lives.

The third classmate, Jakob Ehrat, was so fascinated by Einstein that he wrote:

> He refused to appear other than he was. He took not the slightest trouble, on speculative grounds, to hide certain Jewish characteristics which were natural to him and made relationships with Christians difficult. In early youth he had already freed himself as far as possible from the judgments and prejudices of his fellow man. In religious matters, too, this incorruptible, undogmatic and inwardly so balanced scientist would have nothing to do with obscurities. I never saw a trace of pettiness, the slightest weakening in his courage for truth and in his refusal to compromise. His almost prophetic gift for justice, his inner strength and spontaneous feeling for beauty impressed me so much that I often dreamed of him long after life had separated us. And each time on awakening I felt grieved that my meeting with him again was only a dream.

Several years after graduation, the fourth student, Louis Kollros, a member of the faculty at the Polytechnical School, did everything possible to help Einstein secure a professorship at the same institution.

At the beginning of his undergraduate studies Einstein met the Jewish-Italian engineer Michele Angelo Besso—a perennial student, a highstrung Italian Jew with a critical mind. They met at the home of a musical friend where they both went to play the violin. Besso, six years older than Einstein, came to the engineering branch of the Polytechnical School from the University of Rome. It was Besso who introduced Einstein to the work of Ernst Mach, the physicist and philosopher whose skeptical attitude toward the basic concepts of classical mechanics strengthened Einstein's own inner skepticism and keen mind and initiated his thinking about the special theory of relativity. (Ernst Mach is best known for his experiments on the flow of air over a moving object as it reaches the speed of sound. Later the speed of sound in air was called mach 1, twice the speed of sound mach 2, and so on.) Even though Einstein was influenced by Mach's views of classical mechanics, Mach could never accept the current atomic theory or the theory of relativity. Besso, like Grossmann, became a close friend and was acknowledged in the 1905 paper on special relativity. Over a period of 52 years they exchanged at least 229 letters.

Two people saw Einstein daily and were impressed by his personal qualities—his landlady, Mrs. Markwalder, and her daughter, Susanne. When they moved to a different house, Einstein moved with them. He enjoyed playing the violin while Susanne accompanied him on the piano. She observed:

During this period he was already preparing for his examinations, but he seldom mentioned them. He had no qualms that he would not pass. Formal people and official society for whom one had to put on one's Sunday best were anathema to him. He avoided them whenever he could. In mild weather he often used to sit on the verandah smoking his pipe, watching the sunset or the stars. He never annoyed my mother except when he forgot the house door key, which incidentally he was constantly doing. The doorbell would ring at the most impossible hours in the night and she would be awakened by the cry, "It's Einstein. I've forgotten my key again." His impulsive and upright nature, however, was so irresistible that she never took long to forgive him. When he returned from his holidays in Milan he used to stand rather uncouthly in the doorway and say, "Will you have me back again or are you going to chuck me out?"

Einstein could also be blunt. Miss Markwalder said that once, when he was playing the violin and she the piano,

A widow who lived above us asked my mother whether she could come down to our drawing room with her two daughters and listen to our practice. After some hesitation she agreed. When the three lovers of music took their seats on the sofa and began to rattle their long knitting needles and to disturb our performance with an occasional sigh over dropped stitches, Einstein ostentatiously closed my score and put his violin back in its case. When the eldest visitor asked, "What, are you stopping so soon?" he replied sarcastically, "Oh, we would not dream of disturbing your work."

Comparison

A certain sameness marked the college years of Newton and Einstein. They enrolled at good universities, although neither man attended the best college available at the time. In Newton's day, the training in mathematics was better at Oxford and in London than at Cambridge, and, in Einstein's day, the German universities gave the best instruction in physics. Outside of Germany the Polytechnical School in Zurich was one of the best places to learn physics. The major reason for Einstein's choice of Zurich was that, remembering the experience at the Gymnasium, he did not want to attend college in Germany.

Both boys were exposed to excellent mathematicians. Each was a good student but not at the top of his class. Neither one worked for grades or established any scholastic records, and their parents could not brag about their sons' achievements. However, Newton and Einstein worked hard. They were graduate-type students from the day they entered college and became immersed in self-education. Newton made a great contribution to mathematics in his senior year by developing the binomial theorem. Before graduation, Einstein was already questioning the accepted foundations of physics.

A few people recognized Newton's and Einstein's talents. Newton had the admiration of his teachers, Einstein of his classmates.

3

Exile from Academic Life

Newton was 22 and Einstein 21 when they received their first college degrees. Until then their lives were similar in many ways, but the most obvious similarities were yet to come. Neither could continue with college. Each man's education was interrupted, although for different reasons. However, their subsequent paths were the same. Because of the plague, the University of Cambridge was closed for two years, and Newton returned to the family's farm in Woolsthorpe. Einstein tried hard but unsuccessfully to obtain an assistantship in a university. His good grades in the examinations were useless. Even at the lowest level there was no opening for him.

During their exile from university life, totally on their own and away from help and stimulation by others, the creativity of these two giants soared. The magnitude, variety, and originality of their accomplishments have never been equaled. Yet their greatest intellectual achievements, destined to establish the highest level of abstract thought, did not come until several years later.

Newton

Newton left Cambridge on August 1, 1665. He returned for three months in the spring of 1666, but then he went back to Woolsthorpe where he stayed until March 25, 1667. Perhaps he visited Cambridge briefly in the interval. In the quiet of exile, Newton made spectacular discoveries in three distinct subjects —calculus, light, and gravitation. During his seventies, he looked back and remarked, "In those days I was in the prime of my age for invention, and minded mathematics and physics more than at any time since."

First thoughts on the calculus came in Newton's junior year in college. But it was during the year of the plague that he wrote his original papers on both differential and integral calculus. Using differential calculus, he became the first to handle routinely the mathematics of rate of change. His development of integral calculus enabled him to describe areas under a curve. He was so pleased with his ability to find the area of a hyperbola that, for one problem, he carried his calculations out to 52 significant figures.

Newton showed that white light could be diffracted by a prism and separated into different colors. He also showed that colors could be recombined to give white light. Newton worked at the difficult task of grinding lenses from nonspherical surfaces.

Because of chromatic aberration, that is, the refraction of different colors to different foci, he decided that it would not be worthwhile to make increasingly larger telescopes of the type then generally in use. Since chromatic aberration was not produced by reflected light, an instrument equipped with concave mirrors instead of lenses had real advantages. Although at least two other men suggested constructing a reflecting telescope for reasons different from his, Newton made the first one. He found a need for the instrument on theoretical grounds and laid plans for making it while on the farm. Later he cast and polished the mirrors and made his own alloy. Several years afterwards, an English optician, John Dolland, overcame the defects of chromatic aberration by making two-piece lenses of different kinds of glass having compensating properties. Today's telescopes use mirrors or lenses.

Newton's feats in originating the calculus and exploring the properties of light were topped by his development of the theory which explained gravitational attraction. In his day it was clear that the earth attracted bodies near it's surface. The possibility, however, that gravitational forces extended beyond the surface had not been seriously considered. While in a contemplative mood on the farm, mulling over the pull required to hold the moon in its path, he saw an apple fall to the ground (not on his head). Did the same gravitational pull that the earth had for the apple extend to the moon only reduced by distance? Did the apple attract the earth as the earth attracted the apple with the difference in force related to the differences in mass of the two bodies? Newton proposed his inverse square law of universal gravitation, but he kept his deductions to himself for many years. To firmly establish the law that the attractive force between two bodies varies directly as the product of their mass and inversely as the square of the distance between them, he had to show that the gravitational pull of a spherical earth is the same as it would be if the whole mass were concentrated at the center. This he could not do until later.

Thus, in two years Newton fathered the field of theoretical physics and, with almost no equipment, made his mark as an experimental physicist.

Einstein

Einstein's enforced separation from university life was longer than Newton's, and the first two years were anything but tranquil. His monthly allowance ceased, and he went through a succession of temporary jobs: carrying out calculations for an astronomer, teaching at high schools, and tutoring privately. He said that playing the violin with his music-minded friends kept him from going to pieces. In spite of these handicaps, Einstein's knack for thermodynamics and statistics, plus his intensive self-training before and during college, enabled him to study seriously. Within a year after graduation, he published a paper on capillary action. He also thought about getting a PhD degree. But the next year was difficult. He tried to cope with the agonizing loss of his father, who had been severely ill for some time. Einstein kept studying, however, and published two papers on thermodynamics.

With Marcel Grossmann's help, Einstein obtained a minor but secure post at the Swiss patent office in Berne. Two years later he was, in turn, able to assist Michele Besso in getting a job in the same department. At this "cobbler's job" of examining patents, Einstein saved time to work out his own ideas in physics. His outside intellectual pursuits were intense. He and his friends, Maurice Solovine and Conrad Habicht, met informally but regularly to scrutinize the works of philosophers. Their meetings, which they designated in jest as the "private

Berne Academy," stimulated Einstein and served as a sounding board for his ideas. His friend and co-worker, Michele Besso, also listened attentively to Einstein. Other people became aware of his talents. When Dr. Heinrich Zangger of Zurich University wanted help in solving a problem in applied mathematics, he was advised to see Albert Einstein in Berne. Dr. Zangger gained Einstein's help, recognized his genius, and supported Einstein whenever he could. It was during this period that Einstein married Mileva Maric, and that their first child was born.

After two years at the patent office Einstein completed his monumental works on relativity, mass-energy relationships, and atomic theory. Before publication of his findings in 1905 (when he was only 26 years old), he had not even seen a theoretical physicist except, as Infeld said, "when he looked in the mirror." A bright, eager, persistent nobody came up with the solutions to important problems in physics and revolutionized space-time concepts for the first time since Newton.

Einstein's publications in 1905 covered many subjects and included a PhD thesis. Among the most notable was the special theory of relativity. For almost ten years, he had asked himself about the speed of light as it might be measured by observers traveling at different velocities. He found that time and space always must be considered as part of a unified concept and not as unrelated factors. When the speed of light is assumed to be the same for all observers, then both mass and time are influenced by motion.

Einstein derived the equation $E = mc^2$. He showed clearly that energy and mass are related and set the theoretical groundwork for the development of atomic energy.

Einstein extended the quantum theory of heat radiation,

which had been developed by Max Planck in 1900, to include light as well as all forms of radiant energy. He explained the photoelectric effect and helped lay the basis for quantum mechanics.

He neatly showed that if the atomic theory of matter holds, small particles suspended in a liquid should exhibit a zig-zag motion. Einstein predicted the motion through his mastery of statistics before recognizing that the phenomenon was the same as Brownian movement.

Comparison

A story had been told about an aspiring musician of 20 who sought Mozart's assistance in composing a symphony. Mozart reviewed the score and asked, "Why do you begin with a symphony as one of your first efforts? It is much better to start with something small, perhaps a sonata."

The man looked puzzled and answered, "It is surprising to hear you say this when you composed your first symphony at only 16."

"I know," replied Mozart, "but I didn't have to ask for help."*

Einstein and Newton did not ask for help. When their graduate work was interrupted, they studied alone, developed independent ideas, and persisted with and completed self-assigned projects in conceptual thought. Each had an unerring grasp of the essential in relating time, motion, space, energy, mass, light, and gravity. Newton gave a clear identity to *mass* and Einstein to *time*.

Newton's peaceful exile made possible two years of fervid

*In fact, Mozart wrote his first symphony as a child of 8 and probably was helped by his father, a musician.

work on theoretical problems. He also was resourceful and skillful enough to perform experiments. Einstein's separation from university life was longer—nine years. The first two years were dreary. Yet he managed to publish three papers and play the violin with friends. The next two years were comparable to Newton's period at Woolsthorpe. The patent office provided serene, steady employment. The work was not a chore because he quickly understood the workings of an invention. However, unlike Newton, whose time was totally his own, Einstein carved minutes for research out of his daily routine as a civil servant with a family to support. Newton had time; Einstein made time. Einstein's fame rests on his accomplishments and also on the personal aspects of his life. Here was a scientist the layman could identify with—a boy who got into trouble at school, who failed a college entrance test, and who could not get a university appointment. On the basis of great ability and drive, he surpassed the physicists of his day.

Einstein and Newton shared a remarkable habit. Each man wrote constantly, committing his thoughts to paper in an organized manner. A major difference was that Einstein published his ideas unhesitatingly. Newton did not.

4

Mature Scientists

Newton in 1667 and Einstein in 1905 were young but already seasoned scientists. However, they were recognized as outstanding by only the few peers who knew them and anticipated their continuing success. Newton's *Philosophiae Naturalis Principia Mathematica*, or the *Principia*, published at the age of 44 in 1687, and Einstein's *The Foundation of the General Theory of Relativity*, published at the age of 37 in 1916, were their intellectual masterpieces. After these reports, Newton and Einstein were known throughout the world. Each became a legend within his lifetime. Newton's productive career following the period of exile lasted 20 years. Afterward he ceased doing original work in science.

Einstein's work continued after 1916. Within a year he produced a classic paper on radiation that was to be the cornerstone for the development of the laser beam. He became, as one mathematician said, "the first two most outstanding physicists of his day." Einstein was the leader in theoretical physics until 1925. His great scientific output, like Newton's, continued for 20 years following his first major accomplishments. But after 1925, Einstein persisted in theoretical research in a separate and independent direction from that of most other physicists. The significance of the work he did during his last 30 years is still unknown.

Newton

A year after Newton returned to Cambridge as a Minor Fellow of Trinity College, he received a Master of Arts degree and the title of Major Fellow. Professor Isaac Barrow, who had recognized Newton's ability as an undergraduate, asked the young man for assistance in a book he was writing on optics. Newton's first honor came from this teacher. Barrow resigned his chair as Lucasian Professor of Mathematics in large part so that Newton, at the age of 26, could have the position. At 29 Newton was elected a Fellow of the Royal Society. He made a second reflecting telescope and presented it to that organization. At 35 Newton was invited to become Master of Trinity College, but, because he was not in holy orders, he could not accept the post.

Until the age of 44, Newton continued his immense productivity. He led an isolated existence but worked constantly. With few teaching obligations, no family responsibilities, and little traveling, Newton devoted himself to mathematics, chemistry, physics (both experimental and theoretical), and theology. When he was about 36 years old, Newton began to complain that working in science was tiring and that the subject was barren and difficult. Still, his compulsion for seeing a project through to completion did not change.

The evolution of the *Principia* reveals much about Newton's character. He was persistent in solving a problem and reluctant to communicate the solution to others, except when persuaded by a friend. Newton, before the age of 24, proposed the inverse square law of gravity. He knew that the law described rather well many aspects of our solar system, but he lacked mathematical proof for two significant points: one, the path of a body acting under this law would be an ellipse; and two, the gravitational pull of a spherical earth would be the same as if the whole mass were concentrated at the center. By the age of 33 he proved the first point, and nine years later, he proved the second. In January 1684, shortly after Newton solved the second problem, Edmund Halley, Robert Hooke, and Sir Christopher Wren were talking together in a London tavern. Like Newton, but after him, each of these brilliant men deduced independently the inverse square law from Kepler's third law of planetary motion. But not one could show that if the law held, the orbit of a planet would be an ellipse. Wren said that he would give a book worth 40 shillings to the one who solved the problem within two months. He did not have to pay the bet. Newton's ability as a mathematician was well known, and Halley decided to go to Cambridge to seek his help. In August 1684, to Halley's surprise and satisfaction, Newton answered without hesitation that the orbit would be an ellipse. Newton also said that he had solved the problem some time ago but could not lay his hands on the proof at that moment. Newton agreed to rework the solution and mail it to Halley. A few weeks later, Halley was ecstatic. Newton had sent him two different proofs for the problem. Halley returned to Cambridge to encourage Newton to extend the work and publish it. More than anyone else, Halley rekindled Newton's waning interest in physics and mathematics. After 18 months of intense labor, the seasoned and mature Newton, at 44, gave Halley the three books that made up the *Principia*. Halley published the books, at his own expense, in July or August of 1687. That is the history of the greatest book of science and the beginning of theoretical physics.

Einstein

Einstein's course did not follow as simple a path as Newton's. A year after the great publications of 1905, the only event in Einstein's life was promotion to expert second-class at the patent office. This change in status had nothing to do with notable findings in science. He published five more papers. The next year was also an ordinary one. His application for a position in the department of theoretical physics at the University of Berne was rejected, and he wrote several more papers. Einstein worked at the patent office, maintained his family, played the violin and piano, invented—with the Habicht brothers—an apparatus to measure small voltages, and made time for his great love, theoretical physics.

By the time Einstein reached his 29th year, events changed. His teacher, Hermann Minkowski, simplified the mathematical form of the special theory of relativity. Einstein was finally accepted at the University of Berne where he gave his first lecture to an audience of four. At 30, after seven years' work as a civil servant at the patent office, he was able to resign and accept a position as associate professor at Zurich University. Support for that appointment came from doctors Zangger and Kleiner at Zurich University and also from physicists outside of Switzerland. Geneva University awarded Einstein his first honorary degree. The unusual quality of Einstein's work was noted by the leading theoretical physicists Planck, Nernst, and Lorentz. Planck said, "It is hardly necessary to mention that this new interpretation of the time concept by Einstein makes the highest demands on the physicist's capacity for abstraction and powers of imagination. In daring it exceeds everything which has yet been achieved in speculative natural science."

When Einstein was 31, his second son was born. At the age of 32, he left Switzerland to become professor of theoretical physics at the German University in Prague. Within 18 months, he returned to Switzerland for a professorship at his alma mater, the Zurich Federal Institute of Technology. The institution that had granted him a degree, but not even the lowest job 11 years earlier, made him a full professor. Again his friend, Marcel Grossmann, who was on the faculty, lent a helping hand. In 1914 at the age of 35, Einstein was appointed to the chair of theoretical physics at the Kaiser Wilhelm Institute in Berlin. For the next 22 years, his position was secure. He no longer was the "gypsy," as he usually called himself.

The general theory of relativity began to unfold in 1907. Einstein studied problems of gravity and unexplained motions of the planet Mercury. Years earlier, he had questioned the correctness of the inverse square law of gravity. He knew that in general the law held empirically, but on theoretical grounds he did not know how such a law could be deduced. He did not want to accept a formulation as a basic law of nature without good reason. From 1907 to 1917, he investigated problems of gravity and light. In 1916 the complete version of the general theory of relativity, which is really a theory of gravitation, was published. Parts of this thesis appeared before the final report. In fact, the theory was first put forth by Einstein and Grossmann in 1912, but an error had led them astray. Marcel Grossmann introduced Einstein to the tensor calculus and Reimann geometry and assisted with the extremely complicated mathematics. The finished product, completed when Einstein was 37, represented a unique intellectual feat. Since that time, theoretical physics has been intimately associated with the most advanced mathematics.

Consistent with the new theory was the motion of the planet Mercury. However, agreement between theory and observation was considered only a minimum requirement. After all, one could devise a theory to agree with a single known experimental finding. A better test for Einstein's theory of gravitation would be to measure a physical property, consistent with the deductions, that had not been detected previously. According to the new view, a gravitational field should have an effect on radiation. For example, light from stars passing near the sun en route to earth should be deflected slightly.

In 1919 a British expedition led by Arthur Eddington set out to photograph stars visible during a solar eclipse on May 29. The expedition consisted of two groups. One went to Principe on the West African Gulf of Guinea and the other to Sobral in Brazil. Only Eddington's group at Principe was lucky enough at the last minute to have satisfactory weather for taking adequate pictures. By late autumn, analyses of the data were complete. At a meeting of the Royal Society in London, on the evening of November 6, Eddington announced that light from the stars was deflected to the extent predicted by Einstein's general theory of gravitation. At that meeting, the famous physicist, J. J. Thompson, said that Einstein's work was "perhaps the greatest achievement in the history of human thought." Newspaper releases the following morning brought him suddenly to the view of the public. His name became a household word. The physicist, Max Born, wrote, "I was so impressed by the greatness of his conception that I decided never to work in this field."

In 1917, Einstein had published his classic paper on radiation, which contained the first description of light generated by stimulated emission. On the basis of this work, the laser beam was produced 43 years later in 1960. In 1921 Einstein was awarded the Nobel Prize for his paper of 1905 on the photoelectric effect. In 1924 he helped introduce wave mechanics originated by Louis de Broglie. By 1925 Einstein was a theoretical physicist in a class by himself. After 1925 he departed from the work of most theoretical physicists and, for the next 30 years, worked on his own developing a unified field concept. Never again did he join the mainstream.

During the 20 active years before 1925, Einstein was busy with numerous nonscientific projects. In 1914 he became an active pacifist despite the antipathy toward pacifism in Germany. In 1919 he began to favor a Jewish homeland in Palestine, and he contributed to the success of fund-raising drives. To support these causes and to give lectures on his scientific work, he traveled all over the world. Often Einstein was harassed by crowds who wanted to welcome the scientist or express either antirelativity or anti-Semitic prejudices.

Because of his experience at the patent office and his knowledge of physics Einstein was also often consulted by industrial firms. His family life was complicated by divorce, but whenever possible, he spent the summers with his two sons. Later, Einstein married his cousin, Elsa Einstein Lowenthal.

Comparison

As mature theoretical physicists, Newton at 44 and Einstein at 37 completed the greatest works of abstract thought created by man. The patterns were identical. Two brilliant men, with a feeling for the essential and with great perseverance, made enormous advances. Years later, without letup in determination or drive, they produced their masterpieces. Newton founded theoretical physics. Einstein made theoretical physics inseparable from advanced mathematics. Both were interested primarily in gravity and light. They remained active for nearly 20 years after their first significant achievements.

The scientific work of both men tended to be similar, but their day-to-day living patterns were not. Newton maintained an extremely isolated existence. Nearly all of his time, and he slept little, was devoted to mathematics, experimental and theoretical physics, chemistry, and theology. It is possible that this prolonged solitude was partly responsible for his tiring of science. Einstein constantly fought for time to continue his scientific work. Within four years after graduation, Newton attained an endowed professorship at Cambridge. Einstein wandered for 11 years before his appointment as full professor at his alma mater. He waited another three years before he felt permanently settled. He championed social causes, traveled far, and met many dignitaries. Relaxation came in playing the violin and piano, and in sailing.

5

Famous Men

Original work in science seldom comes easily. Usually an accomplishment results from demanding and sustained effort. While the intense effort is being made, the investigator's personal interest in the project and his feeling for its importance must be so strong that they provide the driving force for him to continue. How long can this effort be continued? Through one major project for most scientists. Through two projects, for a few, but seldom more. Even before working on the *Principia*, Newton complained about the difficulty of continuing in science. He had already completed several major works. He had good insight about his own limitations. Endurance records were no longer for him. He tried to "kick himself upstairs" by finding an administrative post. He did not behave as many scientists do now who, after one or two good pieces of work, give up research, gratefully accept administrative positions, and then outwardly complain that they would do anything to get back into the laboratory.

Einstein's situation was different. He lived through two world wars and their associated political and social upheaval. Although he wanted to continue in his independent way and study the problems of physics full time for the rest of his life, he worried about the large and small problems of mankind. He sensed adverse political and social situations almost instantly and wanted to help. He believed that his fame, which he always felt he did not deserve, should be put to good use.

Newton

In the spring of 1687, at the age of 44, Newton had completed the three books of the *Principia*, but they were a few months away from publication. He then joined a small committee of the Senate at the University of Cambridge to decide the university's stand on a political-religious issue. King James II wanted to bring the universities under Catholic influence. Newton firmly opposed the Crown's wishes. The committee presented their case before the high commission at Westminster but without effect. Because of Newton's efforts, his friends elected him to represent the university in parliament. By the time parliament convened in January 1688, James II had been replaced by William and Mary. Although he spoke little as a member of the House of Commons, Newton dealt effectively with university problems. Thirteen months later, in February 1689, parliament was dissolved. Newton returned to academic solitude at Cambridge.

While parliament was in session in London, Newton met influential and important people, including John Locke and Sam-

uel Pepys. John Locke was perhaps the greatest political philosopher in English history. Locke and Charles Montague, Newton's friend and former student at Trinity, were devoted to
Newton and helped him. Montague was brilliant and ambitious.
In college his major interests were literary studies, but he also
was talented in science. He first married his uncle's widow, ten
to twenty years his senior, and the mother of nine children.
Later he became the common-law husband of Newton's step-
niece, Catharine Barton. Montague was named, in succession,
Earl of Halifax, Chancellor of the Exchequer, and finally,
President of the Royal Society.

Shortly before parliament dissolved, Newton's friends persuaded the King to appoint him Provost of King's College in
Cambridge. Unfortunately for Newton, and certainly for King's
College, the appointment was proposed at a time when the
college was stiffening its opposition to the Crown's control of
university affairs. The application failed. Montague, Locke and
others continued their efforts to secure a good administrative
position for Newton but without success. In 1691 Locke suggested Newton for Master of Charterhouse, a secondary school
in London, but Newton rejected the offer. Newton would have
accepted a position as Comptroller of the Mint, but Locke
failed in his attempt to get him the post.

The years from 1691 to 1696 were difficult, emotionally, for
Newton. Before his 50th birthday, he suffered a severe nervous
breakdown. But he managed to maintain his correspondence
on mathematical problems. Finally in 1696, with Montague as
Chancellor of the Exchequer and President of the Royal Society, and with continued backing by Locke, Newton was made
Warden of the Royal Mint. After ten years of waiting, he got
what he wanted — a dignified, nonscientific position. For a time,

he was able to retain his Cambridge fellowship and Lucasian professorship. In 1699, the day after his 57th birthday, Newton was promoted to Master of the Mint, a post he kept until death. Several times he was offered large gifts and pensions which he always declined: "I will have no pension."

On December 10, 1701, Newton resigned his Lucasian professorship and, soon after, his fellowship. In the same year the university honored him again by electing him to serve as their representative in parliament. In 1702, however, after parliament dissolved, he refused to run again. In 1703 he became President of the Royal Society and was elected every year thereafter until he died 24 years later. In April 1705 he was knighted by Queen Anne and became the first scientist in England to receive the honor. After being knighted, Newton spent a lot of time and money establishing his pedigree and was finally successful in linking his background to the British peerage.

How would a brilliant scientist who lived the life of a recluse, spoke little, had few exchanges with men, was suspicious and easily offended, and who had suffered a nervous breakdown make out as an executive? Obviously many people today would not offer a top executive post unrelated to science to such a person. The fact is that Newton did well. He was practical and had excellent judgment. Conscientious, steady, firm, and fair, he dealt effectively with graft, corruption, and personal disputes. He handled men well and knew how to balance difficult situations. He was a conservative, not a revolutionary. In short, Newton was at the very least an excellent executive and may have been outstanding. Besides taking care of the numerous routine problems of the mint, he brought in an officer for legal work. He also required that coins be struck at their individual right weights. In his 31 years as a public servant at the Royal

Mint, he saw five wardens and four comptrollers enter office. During that period Newton invested wisely and became a wealthy man.

Newton's existence in London was, for the most part, tranquil. Personal difficulties, however, arose with Robert Hooke and John Flamsteed and did not end until the deaths of Hooke in 1703 and Flamsteed in 1720. Much more important was the international controversy between Newton and Leibniz on the origin of the calculus. They both claimed the achievement. Perhaps the most famous of scientific disputes, it lasted many years, gradually wearing itself out.

During his governmental service away from Cambridge, Newton pursued his work in theology and science and discussed religious problems with Locke and other men. Some of his manuscripts were put into definitive form. In science he remained alert but avoided doing original theoretical work.

When Newton came home from the mint on January 26, 1697, he received a challenge from Johann Bernoulli. The Swiss mathematician had proposed two problems for solution. Characteristically, Newton skipped supper and sleep and stayed with the problems until 4:00 A.M. when his answers were complete. Only Leibniz and one other mathematician had solved them. Newton's explanations were published without his name, as he had requested. On seeing the solutions, however, Bernoulli remarked, "The lion is known by his claw." In 1716, at the age of 74, Newton received another problem to solve. This one came from Leibniz, and, as before, Newton received it when he returned from the mint. As he had done 19 years earlier, he solved the problem in a few hours, missing supper and sleep.

In August 1699, Newton exhibited at the Royal Society a sextant that he had invented and made himself. In 1701 he described a thermometer which he had worked on earlier. Later in 1704, he presented to the society a burning glass of seven lenses that he had made. Newton published his *Opticks* in 1704 and followed it with revised editions in 1718, 1721, and 1726, a few months before his death. He helped prepare new editions of the *Principia* that appeared in 1713 and 1726.

After a full and productive life, Newton died on March 20, 1727. Before burial in Westminster Abbey, his body lay in state in the Jerusalem Chamber. The Lord High Chancellor, two dukes, and three earls supported the pall. His monument was located in a space that previously had been refused to nobility. The occasion of Newton's funeral was the first and only time that such national honors were accorded a man of science, learning, or art in England.

Einstein

In 1925 at the age of 46, Einstein began to work apart from the main trend in physics. He concentrated on gravity and the unified field theory. He remained totally dedicated to finding a formulation that would unite in one concept the workings of nature on both a molecular and a cosmic scale. Excerpts from letters written during his last years show that Einstein continued his work in physics. On January 6, 1951, he wrote to his old friend, the Queen Mother of Belgium, "I am done with fiddling. With the passage of years, it has become more and more unbearable for me to listen to my own playing. I hope you have not suffered a similar fate. What has remained is the relentless work on difficult scientific problems. The fascinating magic of that work will continue to my last breath."

On December 27, 1952, he wrote to a friend in England, "My

work keeps me under constant tension as before even though imagination and endurance have slackened." In 1953, at 74, he published his final paper on the unified field theory. Although he was sure of the mathematics, he was less certain of the physical concepts.

In addition to original papers in physics, Einstein wrote several sketches on the scientific achievements of famous men including Isaac Newton, James Clerk Maxwell, H. A. Lorentz, Max Planck, Walter Nernst, Thomas A. Edison, and Albert A. Michelson.

From 1925 to 1955 Einstein was fortunate in having bright graduate students or assistants who later distinguished themselves: Leo Szilard, Leopold Infeld, Cornelius Lanczos, Nathan Rosen, W. Mayer, J. Grommer, John G. Kemeny, Peter G. Bergmann, V. Bargmann, E. G. Straus, and Bruria Kaufman.

In 1928 Helen Dukas, an alert, objective young woman, began working as Einstein's private secretary and office manager. After Elsa Einstein's death, she also became his housekeeper. She shared Einstein's regard for truth and worked with him until he died 27 years later. Originally from a large, German-Jewish family in Freiburg *im* Breisgau, she now lives in Einstein's house in Princeton with his stepdaughter, Margot. Since Einstein's death, she and Otto Nathan have managed Einstein's literary estate. More than anyone else, Helen Dukas assisted Einstein during the last third of his life.

Before 1925 Einstein had received many honors—degrees from the universities of Geneva and Princeton, the Barnard Medal for Science from Columbia, the Royal Society's Copley Medal, and the Nobel Prize. In the last thirty years of his life, he continued to receive honors: degrees from his alma mater, the Zurich Federal Institute of Technology; and also from

Cambridge in 1930, Oxford in 1931, and Harvard in 1935. In 1955 element 99, detected in the debris after the atom bomb test of October 1952, was named einsteinium.

From 1925 to 1933, Einstein traveled from Berlin to South America, Switzerland, France, Belgium, the Netherlands, England, and the United States. He went to each of these countries twice except for South America, which he visited only once. He attended scientific meetings and took part in the discussions by the Committee of Intellectual Cooperation of the League of Nations in Geneva. Einstein became a member of the Board of Directors of the German League for Human Rights, a pacifist movement.

During his travels, Einstein met Queen Elizabeth of Belgium, Winston Churchill, David Lloyd George, George Bernard Shaw, Arturo Toscanini, Fritz Kreisler, John D. Rockefeller, Jr., Helen Keller, Upton Sinclair, Charlie Chaplin, Clarence Darrow, and many other celebrities.

From 1915 to 1925, Einstein had been actively involved with pacifist groups as well as with supporting the Jewish people. In the early 1930s, Einstein made two important decisions. On board ship in December 1931, he wrote, "I decided today that I shall essentially give up my Berlin position." He had been at the Kaiser Wilhelm Institute for 17 years. From many offers, he accepted a position at the Institute for Advanced Study in Princeton.

The second major decision concerned his feelings about pacifism. Before Hitler achieved full power, Einstein saw what was going to happen. "I am a dedicated but not an absolute pacifist! This means that I am opposed to the use of force under any circumstances, except when confronted by an enemy who pursues the destruction of life as an end in itself." He repeatedly warned the world that Germany was preparing for war.

Einstein was caught between criticism by pacifist groups and vicious, verbal attacks and threats from the Nazis. On September 9, 1933, he wrote from England to Miss Dukas in Belgium, "The antimilitarists attack me as being an evil renegade. These fellows wear blinders; they refuse to acknowledge their expulsion from 'paradise'." During this difficult period he lost two of his closest friends: Hendrik Lorentz died of natural causes at 75 in 1928, and Lorentz's associate and successor, Paul Ehrenfest, killed himself at 57 in 1933.

In 1932, at the suggestion of the League of Nations, Einstein addressed an open letter to Freud on the causes and prevention of war. Within a few months, the 74-year-old Freud replied. These letters are presented in full in Appendix A at the end of this volume.

Einstein left England for America in October, 1933. He never returned to Europe.

The years from 1933 to 1955, when Einstein was at Princeton, encompassed the tragedy of World War II (September 1, 1939 to August 14, 1945), as well as its prologue and aftermath. Einstein put forth a great effort to help refugees from Europe and to support the United States during the war. He granted many interviews and wrote articles. At the age of 55 in 1934, he gave a violin recital in New York City to raise funds for scientists fleeing from Germany. To obtain money for a United States War Bond drive in 1943, Einstein copied by hand the 30 printed pages of his original paper of 1905 on the theory of relativity. The manuscript was auctioned and sold for $6 million and is now in the Library of Congress in Washington, D.C. Many of Einstein's numerous writings on world problems are included in the excellent book, *Einstein on Peace*, by Otto Nathan and

Heinz Norden.

In 1936 Einstein's wife, Elsa, died. His stepdaughter, Ilse, had died two years earlier. Marcel Grossmann, the brilliant college classmate who helped Einstein so much, also died in 1936 in Zurich. Such personal losses, added to the sadness of world affairs, contributed to Einstein's loneliness.

In 1939, at the beginning of World War II, Einstein signed a letter, drafted by others, which helped open the way for the development of the atomic bomb. Because of its great importance, this subject must be described as accurately as possible.

Leo Szilard, Enrico Fermi, Eugene P. Wigner, Victor F. Weisskopf, and Edward Teller were some of the physicists anxious to have the United States accelerate atomic research because they feared that Germany was probably doing just that. By March 1939, Szilard, Fermi, and others showed that a self-sustaining chain reaction to produce atomic energy might be possible. Attempts by Szilard and Fermi to interest the United States Navy in these developments were unsuccessful. Szilard alone retained a sense of urgency.

By early summer, Szilard and Wigner were apprehensive that Germany might obtain large quantities of uranium from the Belgian Congo. Because Szilard knew that Einstein was a friend of Queen Elizabeth of Belgium, he and Wigner went to see Einstein on July 15, 1939, at Nassau Point, Peconic, Long Island, to request that he write to the Queen. Also, Wigner wanted additional uranium for the United States. Together they drafted a letter to the Queen, which was to be submitted first to the State Department for approval. After the visit with Einstein, Szilard talked to Dr. Alexander Sachs, an economist and unofficial advisor to President Roosevelt, about the large sums of money needed for atomic research. During the meeting,

Albert Einstein in his 60s in Princeton, New Jersey. Photograph by
Lotte Jacobi

Sir Isaac Newton. Mezzotint by James MacArdel after the painting
by Enoch Seeman

Woolsthorpe Manor, birthplace of Isaac Newton

The sundial made by Isaac Newton as a boy

King's School in Grantham

Isaac Barrow (1630-1677), the first Lucasian Professor of Mathematics at Cambridge and Newton's teacher. He recognized his pupil's talent and resigned his chair so that Newton could succeed him.

Albert Einstein at the age
of 5 in Munich, Germany

The entrance to Einstein's apartment in Milan

Albert Einstein, a 16-year-old student in Aarau, Switzerland

Max Planck (1858-1947) originated the quantum theory with his publication of 1900, the year Einstein was graduated from college. Einstein's application of Planck's work to light firmly established the quantum theory. Planck, in turn, called attention to Einstein's new concepts and later helped secure his appointment as professor.

The "Berne Academy"—Conrad Habicht, Maurice Solovine, and Albert Einstein

Marcel Grossmann (1878-1936), the astute, irreproachable student and friend of Einstein. He was the first to recognize Einstein's great talent. Use of classroom notes made it possible for Einstein to skip classes and study many aspects of physics and philosophy of his own choice. After college Grossmann again saved Einstein by getting him a job at the patent office when no university would give him a position. Later he assisted with the mathematics of the General Theory of Relativity and helped make it possible for Einstein to return to Zurich from Prague. Einstein's PhD thesis was dedicated "to my friend Dr. Marcel Grossmann."

Einstein at the age of 26 in 1905. In this year he proposed the equation $E = mc^2$, introduced the theory of relativity, explained the photo-electric effect, and described Brownian movement.

Charles Montague (Lord Halifax) (1661-1715), Newton's student and good friend, helped Newton obtain the position at the mint.

The reflecting telescope made by Newton at the age of 29 in 1671

Edmond Halley (1656-1742) persuaded Newton to write the *Principia* and, though he had a family to support and only a modest income, paid for its publication. From a portrait by Thomas Murray

Walther H. Nernst (1864-
1941), physical chemist and
friend of Einstein who, with
Planck, arranged for Ein-
stein to come to Berlin

Einstein's summer home near Berlin

Arrival in America. Einstein's first trip to the United States was in 1921. On board ship in New York harbor, Einstein stands with Ben Zion Mossinson, principal of Jaffe College; Chaim Weizmann, president of the World Zionist Organization; and Menachem, M. Ussishkin, a prominent Zionist.

In February 1923 Einstein visited with the staff of the Technion Institute in Haifa, Palestine. An unidentified man in the photograph sent Einstein the picture with the notation on the back *"Der grösste moment meines Lebens"* (the greatest moment of my life).

Sachs suggested that the Einstein letter be addressed to the president rather than to Queen Elizabeth and said that he would give the letter to Roosevelt personally.

In the last week of July, Szilard, with Teller, visited Einstein again. Einstein agreed with Sachs's proposal and dictated a new draft to Teller. The letter was modified by Szilard, and the final copy was signed by Einstein on August 2, 1939. The letter did not reach the President for two months. The delay occurred because Sachs had been advised by the president's secretary that Roosevelt was very busy, and Sachs also wanted to prepare additional information on the subject for the president. On October 11, 1939, Sachs saw Roosevelt and gave him Einstein's letter with the supporting documents.

Roosevelt wrote to Einstein on October 19. Although Roosevelt acted at once, ensuing action was slow. Sachs took the initiative to keep things going. Szilard and Sachs asked Einstein to write another letter on March 7, 1940, urging more rapid development of atomic energy. Szilard suggested voluntary censorship by physicists in their published reports.

Did these letters do any good in speeding up development of the atomic bomb? Recently some people have stated that the stimuli to work on atomic energy came from a variety of sources, and that even without the letters, the bomb would have been made when it was. Careful analysis, however, suggests that the letters signed by Einstein were, in fact, very important. For a two-year period from 1939 to 1941, the United States lagged behind other countries, such as England, in considering the possibilities of atomic energy. By November 1941, only 16 laboratory projects had been approved for research in atomic energy. The total research allotment was only $300,000.

On June 18, 1942, the army engineers began to play a part,

and on September 17, 1942, General Leslie R. Groves took charge of the Manhattan Project. The letters signed by Einstein must have shortened the initially slow period by six to twelve months. At that time the gulf between science and government was wide. A signature such as Einstein's was needed to stir Roosevelt's imagination. If this slow phase had been prolonged much beyond June 1942, the entire Manhattan Project might not have begun.

The first atom bomb was exploded over Hiroshima on August 6, 1945. When Helen Dukas heard the news on the radio, she rushed to tell Einstein. He was aghast. His immediate remark, "O weh!" was a cry from the heart expressing all the past, present, and future ills of man.

Einstein would not accept any honors from Germany after the war. It was impossible for him to comprehend how the country of his birth, the place where he produced the general theory of relativity, could have carried out its hideous crimes against humanity. For example, Otto Hahn wrote Einstein in 1948 inviting him to become a Foreign Member of the Max Planck Institute which previously had been the Kaiser Wilhelm Institute where Einstein had worked. Einstein declined.

> The crime of the Germans is truly the most abominable ever to be recorded in the history of the so-called civilized nations. The conduct of the German intellectuals—seen as a group—was not better than that of the mob. And even now, there is no indication of any regret or any real desire to repair whatever little may be left to restore after the gigantic murders. In view of these circumstances, I feel an irrepressible aversion to participating in anything which represents any aspects of public life in Germany.

Early in 1951, Einstein rejected an offer to rejoin the Peace Section of the Old Prussian order, *Pour le merité*, with these

words: "Because of the mass murder which the Germans in-
flicted upon the Jewish people, it is evident that a self-respect-
ing Jew could not possibly wish to be associated in any way with
any official German institution. The renewal of my membership is therefore out of the question." In 1950, however, Germany began on a large scale to make amends to those who had
survived and who had suffered loss of health and property.
Subsequent financial aid to Israel was also substantial. In recent
years, highways, schools, and other structures in Germany have
been named for Einstein.

November 9, 1952, marked the death of Einstein's friend,
Chaim Weizmann, chemist and first President of Israel. Suggestions were made that Einstein, then 73, succeed him. Prime
Minister Ben-Gurion instructed Abba Eban, who at that time
was the Israeli Ambassador to the United States, to discuss this
possibility with Einstein. On November 17, 1952, Abba Eban
sent Einstein a telegram. Einstein telephoned Eban that evening
and declined the offer. Here are the texts of the letters exchanged.

Eban to Einstein

Dear Professor Einstein:

I understand the anxieties and doubt which you expressed to
me this evening. On the other hand, whatever your answer, I
am anxious for you to feel that the Prime Minister's question em-
bodies the deepest respect which the Jewish people can repose
in any of its sons. To this element of personal regard, we add the
sentiment that Israel is a small state in its physical dimensions
but can rise to the level of greatness in the measure that it exem-
plifies the most elevated spiritual and intellectual tradition
which the Jewish people have established through its best minds
and hearts both in antiquity and in modern times. Our first

President, as you know, taught us to see our destiny in these perspectives, as you yourself have often exhorted us to do.

Therefore, whatever your response to this question, I hope that you will think generously of those who have asked it and will commend the high purpose and motives which prompted them to think of you at this solemn hour in our people's history.

Yours respectfully,

Abba Eban

Einstein to Eban

Dear Ambassador Eban:

I am deeply moved by the offer from our State of Israel, and at once saddened and ashamed that I cannot accept it. All my life I have dealt with objective matters, hence I lack both the natural aptitude and the experience to deal properly with people and to exercise official functions. For these reasons alone I should be unsuited to fulfill the duties of that high office, even if advancing age were not making increasing inroads on my strength.

I am the more distressed over these circumstances because my relationship to the Jewish people has become my strongest human bond, ever since I became fully aware of our precarious situation among the nations of the world.

Now that we have lost the man who for so many years, against such great and tragic odds, bore the heavy burden of leading us toward political independence, I hope with all my heart that a successor may be found whose experience and personality will enable him to accept the formidable and responsible task.

Albert Einstein

In the early 1950s, as a by-product of fear and the cold war, a severe attack on intellectual freedom was launched by committees established in the Senate and House of Representatives to investigate un-American activities. Einstein vigorously opposed the witch hunt. To emphasize his point, he wrote in 1954, "If I were a young man again and had to decide how to make a living, I would not try to become a scientist, a scholar or a teacher. I would rather choose to be a plumber or a peddler in the hope of finding that modest degree of independence still available under present circumstances."

Einstein had been accused of being a communist many years earlier when he was a member of pacifist groups in Germany. But Einstein was against all forms of dictatorship. During his wide travels he never went to Russia. Einstein objected to the Russian interpretation of "freedom." In 1952 he wrote Dr. Mühsam that over the doorway of the Marx-Lenin Institute of Moscow should be written, "In the realm of truth there is no human authority. Whoever attempts to play the autocrat incurs the laughter of the Gods."

Long before, in September 1933, he had stated, "I am a convinced democrat. It is for this reason that I do not go to Russia although I have received very cordial invitations. My voyage to Moscow would certainly be exploited by the rulers of the Soviets to the profit of their own political aims. Now I am an adversary of Bolshevism just as much as of Fascism. I am against all dictatorships." Einstein was fully committed to the view that only a world government could save people from disaster. He could not visualize a world consisting of independent nationalistic groups with incessant, increasingly destructive wars. His social-political writings were numerous and covered a wide range of topics.

In the last month of his life, Einstein continued working on what was important to him, mainly, world peace through the formation of a world government, problems of the Jewish people, and, of course, physics. His last letter about peace was written to Bertrand Russell on April 11, 1955. The same day he met with the Israeli Ambassador, Abba Eban, to go over notes for a proposed television program related to the forthcoming anniversary of Israel's independence.

On the afternoon of April 13, he collapsed. He died at Princeton Hospital on April 18, 1955. Mathematical equations on which he was working were at his bedside. To honor a request he made earlier, there was no public funeral. A few of his closest friends and relatives gathered in the crematorium in Trenton, New Jersey. Only his executor, the economist Dr. Otto Nathan, said a few words. Einstein's ashes were scattered in a small river. He had stipulated before his death that the location of the river was not to be published. Eventually, his literary estate will go to the Hebrew University in Jerusalem.

Comparison

Both Einstein and Newton committed themselves deeply to public service during the last third of their lives. Newton had a full time executive position at the Royal Mint. Einstein was a member of the academic staff at the Institute for Advanced Study in Princeton. Newton attended to the duties of the mint but continued in science and theology after his daytime job. Einstein, on the other hand, continued studying physics but also took time to work on the problems of establishing peace.

Although Newton did not want to be involved in any disputes, he found himself enmeshed in an international controversy with Leibniz on the origin of the calculus. Einstein, who was by every criterion a devoted pacifist, helped initiate development of the atomic bomb by signing letters to President Roosevelt.

Except for the disputes in science, Newton was satisfied with the last phase of his life. Einstein was apprehensive about the sociological and political problems of the world.

Both men received almost every possible honor. Each lived as an historic figure in his own lifetime, with this difference: Newton fostered the recognition; Einstein did not. Their great capacities for work and clear thinking remained to the end. During their own times and after their deaths, they were the most famous of all scientists.

Even though the full support of their own people helped Einstein and Newton greatly, only Einstein has had schools, colleges, hospitals, and highways named after him. The English, except for naming the recent telescope at the Royal Greenwich Observatory after Isaac Newton, continue to be remiss in recognizing him as they do their statesmen and military heroes. Neither Cambridge nor Oxford has a Newton college. No large highways or buildings are named for him. However, there is a Newton pub, in addition to the new telescope.

PART II

LIFE PATTERNS

6

Health

Newton and Einstein enjoyed excellent physical health for most of their long lives. Perhaps good health was essential to carrying out their demanding work.

Newton

A small, frail baby, born prematurely in December, Newton was not expected to live. Yet he grew normally and developed into a healthy child. His manual dexterity was superb. As an adult, Newton was short and thin, with hair almost completely gray at 30. His physical senses were so keen that he was like a fine instrument. His hearing was unusually sharp. In Cambridge at the age of 30, Newton entered the hall of Trinity College and told the other fellows that he heard cannon firing between the English and Dutch fleets in Southwold Bay—over 60 miles away. He concluded correctly that the Dutch were winning because the battle sounds grew louder as the English retreated and the Dutch approached the English coast.

Newton began to put on weight in his fifties, becoming "the chubby man with the long nose." He never wore glasses. Even in his 80s he could read small print by the light of a coal fire. Not until 80 or 81 did his health begin to fail. At that time he developed urine incontinence and subsequently passed a pea-sized renal stone painlessly. A mild attack of gout occurred. In early March 1727, his gout flared. He fatigued easily and was unable to get rid of a severe cough acquired after a cold in the winter. To get fresher air, he left London for Kensington. After the carriage trip, Newton developed violent fits of lower abdominal pain with only short intermissions. Drops of sweat ran down his face. A diagnosis of a stone in the urinary bladder was made. He complained little and tolerated the pain exceptionally well. By the middle of March, he was seriously ill. He died on Monday, March 20, 1727, between one and two o'clock in the morning. He was alert to the end. He had all his teeth but one, and a full head of hair when he died.

The renal stones were probably composed of uric acid and related to his gout, or they were made of calcium. Movement of a stone during the jaunt by carriage to Kensington probably irritated the bladder lining to produce a cystitis. Death could have resulted from one of several complications of the cystitis.

If one assumes that all the medical information about Newton is accurate, which at times is not prudent to do, it is necessary to speculate about two aspects of his health. First, visual acuity changes with age. Because the lens gradually fails to accommodate for distance, presbyopia, the farsightedness of middle age, develops. Newton could not have been an exception to this phenomenon. His eyes protruded; and if he read small print easily in old age, as other biographers have said, Newton probably was myopic or nearsighted. The naturally developing presbyopia could have compensated for his axial myopia to give him near normal vision late in life.

Protuberant eyes, however, suggest another diagnosis rather than myopia. Prematurely gray hair, the inability to sleep, and emotional lability accompany hyperthyroidism. Newton was thin, and it is possible that inadequate food intake rather than hyperthyroidism caused his slender habitus. But hyperthyroidism, if present, might have increased his alertness and even postponed the arteriosclerosis expected with aging.

Little information is available about the medical history of Newton's family. Why his father died at the age of 36 is not known, nor is the age of Newton's mother at his birth or at her death. The majority of Newton's biographers give the year of his mother's death as 1689. However, the Restoration Register of the Colsterworth Church, examined in June 1967 by the Reverend V. S. Daws, showed that "Mrs. Hannah Smith, Wid. was buried in woollen June ye 4th 1679."* No burial is recorded for a Mrs. Hannah Smith in 1689.

In 1679 when Newton was 36, his half-brother, Benjamin Smith, suddenly became ill with a high fever. Eventually he recovered. His mother, however, who helped care for him, caught the same illness. After a prolonged fever followed by an eruption of blisters, she died. A reasonable explanation is that the brother had a viral infection which was passed on to the mother. In addition, she probably developed erythema multiforme, a severe allergic reaction to the infection leading to formation of blisters on the skin. Her deterioration and death

---

*"Burial in woollen" refers to the woolen shroud required by Charles II's Acts 18 and 19 to encourage the manufacture of wool.

followed. Newton nursed his mother 24 hours a day, changing the dressings over the blisters during her final illness.

Einstein

Einstein was born in March. Although slow in beginning to talk, he developed normally and entered school at the usual age. His health in childhood was excellent. He was of medium height, muscular, brown eyed, and of olive complexion. His father's coloring was darker. After being graduated from college at 22, Einstein became a Swiss citizen and, consequently, a candidate for military service. He was considered unfit, however, because of flat feet and varicose veins. Graying of his hair began at the age of 36 and increased notably by 50. As he aged, his hair also became thinner. His molar teeth were replaced by a bridge.

In adult life, Einstein experienced minor gastrointestinal distress, such as diarrhea, and eating fatty foods was difficult. At the age of 38, while living alone in Berlin, he became seriously ill with abdominal pain and lost much weight. The diagnosis was acute gall-bladder disease. After several weeks in bed, he recovered but felt weak for several months. Einstein then remained well until the age of 49 when a combination of events requiring great physical exertion led to a temporary physical collapse. While sailing far out on a lake, the wind stopped, and Einstein had a difficult time rowing the boat to shore. Not long afterwards he carried heavy luggage over slippery snow at a high altitude. A diagnosis was made of acute enlargement of the heart requiring bed rest for three months and a low-salt diet. Smoking was forbidden and visitors were kept to a minimum. After several months he recovered.

Einstein's physician friend, Dr. Janos Plesch, said, "At first glance he looks fleshy but in fact his build is muscular and quite powerful. He is capable of considerable physical effort and there is nothing wrong with him at all apart from minor stomach troubles and once an acute dilation of the heart brought on by excessive physical effort." But Einstein did have recurrent abdominal pain, partly because of gall bladder disease.

At the age of 69, abdominal cramps began and increased in frequency. Examination revealed a small umbilical hernia and a separate abdominal mass thought to be an aneurysm. The possibility of intestinal obstruction because of a tumor also was considered. Radiographic studies of the gastrointestinal tract were not satisfactory. Electrocardiograms, blood pressure, and blood cholesterol were normal. An exploratory laparatomy, performed by Dr. Rudolf Nissen in December 1948, disclosed the previously suspected hernia and a large aneurysm of the abdominal aorta secondary to arteriosclerosis. The aneurysm was intact, but perforation was only a matter of time. Other findings included an intestinal loop bound to the abdominal wall by an adhesive band and some hepatic enlargement. Dr. Nissen repaired the hernia, cut the adhesion, and Einstein recovered without difficulty.

During the last five years of his life, Einstein suffered from recurrent abdominal pain, usually associated with meals. His symptoms probably were related to pressure from the large aneurysm. Although Einstein had extensive arteriosclerosis, he was mentally active and alert. In 1953 when replacement of part of the aorta became technically feasible, Dr. Nissen discussed the subject with Einstein. But Einstein made it clear that he would never consent to such a procedure. In November 1954, Einstein developed hemolytic anemia following a virus infection. His legs seemed weak, he tired easily and felt tightness in his chest when walking. He responded to treatment with cortisone for one month.

Early in 1955, Einstein sensed that the end was not far away. On February 5, 1955, he wrote to a friend in England: "And yet, to one bent by age death will come as a release; I feel this quite strongly now that I have grown old myself and have come to regard death like an old debt, at long last to be discharged."

On March 31, 1955, Einstein developed severe, colicky pain in the lower left and upper right quadrants of the abdomen. His physician, Dr. Guy K. Dean, gave him an injection of demerol to keep him comfortable. Four additional doses were injected in the following two weeks. During the evening of Tuesday, April 12, 1955, Einstein complained of unusual discomfort in his back.

The next morning he was visited in turn by Dr. Plesch and Abba Eban's associate, Reuven Dafni, the Israeli Consul. He felt terribly tired after the guests left. He ate lunch and went to bed. Approximately two hours later, Einstein collapsed. The aortic aneurysm had ruptured. Dr. Dean made a house call to examine Einstein and saw how ill he was. Two of Dr. Dean's colleagues in the Princeton area, Dr. Ralph J. Belford, a surgeon, and Dr. Willard G. Rainey, an internist, also arrived for consultation. Later in the day, Dr. Gustav Bucky and his son, Dr. Thomas Bucky, came to see Einstein and to decide with Dr. Dean what should be done.

The next day, Thursday, the Buckys returned to Princeton together with Dr. Frank Glenn, a cardiovascular surgeon from Cornell Medical School, and Dr. Rudolf R. Ehrmann, for further consultations. To repair the ruptured, sclerotic patch of the aorta would require a large graft that might encroach upon the renal arteries. There had to be a real desire by the patient to accept such a difficult procedure. As in the earlier discussion with Dr. Nissen, Einstein was not interested. He felt that he was old and that he had already accomplished what he was supposed to do on earth. He was not afraid of dying and thought it senseless to prolong his life.

On Friday, April 15, Dr. Dean admitted Einstein to the Princeton Hospital. Although very ill, Einstein tried to continue his work. He studied some equations and an unfinished statement for the Israelis. He complained to his son, "If only I had more mathematics." He continued working and was completely alert until his death three days later. Like Newton, Einstein died between one and two o'clock on a Monday morning.

Vascular disease was common in the Einstein family. The father, Hermann, had severe angina and died of heart disease at the age of 54. Jakob, Hermann's younger brother and business partner, also died of heart disease at about the same age. Einstein had remarked that many males in his family succumbed to heart disease in their fifties. His sister, Maja, had severe arteriosclerosis. As a youngster, she developed nephritis following scarlet fever and then severe hypertension. After being bedridden for five years because of recurrent cerebral hemorrhages, she died of a stroke. Einstein's son, Hans Albert Einstein, died after a heart attack at age 69; and Eduard, the younger son, died following a stroke at age 55. Einstein's mother was incapacitated for a long time because of metastatic cancer of the uterus, and she died at 62.

Einstein and his wife, Elsa, were more closely related than first cousins. Their mothers were sisters and their fathers first cousins. Elsa's maiden name was Einstein. Except for nearsightedness, which she shared with her mother, she remained in good health until the shock of the death of Ilse, her daughter, in 1934. The circumstances of Ilse's death are not clear, but she had been chronically ill with emotional, gastrointestinal, and endocrine disorders. Within a year, Elsa Einstein developed severe hyperthyroidism. Drug and x-ray therapy were of no avail, and she died in 1936 at the age of 62.

Comparison

The mothers of Einstein and Newton went through the first part of their pregnancies during the late spring and early summer. Despite initial difficulties in development, both boys generally enjoyed excellent health and remained free of physical problems for at least two-thirds of their lives. Their tolerance for pain was great. They lived longer than any of their relatives and were keen and productive to the end.

Einstein was the more robust of the two, but Newton's physical senses were better, being truly outstanding. Einstein had severe arteriosclerosis as he grew older. Newton was surprisingly free from vascular disease. When a young man, Newton may have had hyperthyroidism. Both suffered from gall-bladder disease.

In recent years, much has been said about the association of gout with a high I.Q., and Newton has been cited as an example of this association. Of course, he did have gout and presumably an immeasurably high I.Q. However, his gout appeared so late in life that had he died at 80, the gout would not have been revealed. Einstein did not have gout. Whether or not it would have developed later should not be speculated upon.

7

Personality

Einstein and Newton were men of strong personalities. Agile and independent thinkers, they had unusual similarities and differences. Newton's story is complicated because his endurance records in mathematics, physics, chemistry, and theology culminated in a nervous breakdown. Upon recovery he became a successful executive and, with wise investments, a wealthy man. But Einstein never waivered from his objectives and interests. His dedication to a life free from material possessions and to the understanding of nature was unique.

Newton

Newton's personal needs were few. He was not interested in elaborate dress, food, alcohol, or smoking. A typical breakfast consisted of an orange peel boiled in water and sweetened with sugar, which he drank instead of tea, and bread and butter.

When working on a problem, he often skipped meals. Sometimes he forgot to eat, or he might have for breakfast the supper he missed the previous night. He did not like to waste working time by stopping for meals and frequently ate standing. Apples were a favorite fruit. He might sip a small amount of wine with dinner but otherwise did not drink. Perhaps he smoked a little in his youth but not in later life. After he left Cambridge to work at the mint at the age of 54, he showed greater awareness of his dress and always kept a proper appearance. At that time he also gained much weight.

Newton's only exercise was walking back and forth in his room. Ordinarily he did not join in sports or play chess, although he had the ability to compete. Once in secondary school, he won a broad-jump contest by shrewdly waiting for a gust of wind to propel him. He did not like hunting. Although he sketched animals and copied some poetry as a child, he was not interested in the fine arts. After his first and only evening at an opera, he remarked, "There was too much of a good thing; it was like a surfeit of dinner. The first act I heard with pleasure; the second stretched my patience; at the third I ran away."

Newton's favorite color was red. Nearly everything in his house—all of his furniture, including his bed—was crimson. He did not need entertainment, and to relax he simply switched from one interest to another: mathematics, theoretical physics, experimental physics, chemistry, or theology.

Newton forfeited sleep. Sometimes he could not, or did not want to, sleep. He easily worked 24 hours without stopping. He did not nap during the day, but he did try to sleep at least four or five hours a night because he felt that he needed sleep for emotional stability. His bedtime was usually between 2:00 and

3:00 A.M., although sometimes it was closer to morning. He slept nude.

Newton's steady, unhurried compulsiveness took many forms. He refined his work constantly, but did not use fresh paper for revisions. Scraps and old letters, if handy, were called into service. An odd habit, after grabbing a used page, was to turn the sheet on its side and write over the original lines at right angles. His penmanship was excellent, and he liked to write.

Newton was a mixture of the admirable and difficult—quiet, kind, conscientious, unassuming, independent but not rebellious, he kept to himself and did not have to talk. But he was also serious and seldom laughed, and he worked perpetually and was absentminded. A phenomenal ability to concentrate protected him against distraction. Newton remained close to his immediate family and had several lasting friends. Yet he was sensitive, suspicious, and secretive. Easily irritated and offended, he replied quickly and bluntly. He disliked arguments and went to extremes to avoid them. Although he required no stimulus to complete a project and write it up in a notebook, he usually had to be persuaded to make the information available to others. Not one paper on mathematics was published without prodding. As a young man in Cambridge, Newton permitted Isaac Barrow, the mathematician and teacher, to send some of his early work in mathematics to John Collins, but he stipulated that his name be withheld. Likewise, years later, the solutions of Bernoulli's two problems were published, as Newton requested, without disclosing his name. Except in one or two special instances, he had no desire to simplify his work so that a non-scientist could follow it. He was not a teacher and produced no student of his own in any of the sciences, but he helped at least four talented young mathematicians.

Newton seldom attended church but considered himself religious. After leaving Cambridge for the mint he became more interested in personal and world affairs. He tried to establish his family tree to find out if any relatives were of noble birth. He invested wisely, achieved wealth, and gave generously to family and friends.

After Newton and Miss Storey, Ralf Clark's stepdaughter, broke their engagement, Miss Storey married twice; but she and Newton remained close friends all their lives. Newton became engaged a second time but did not marry. He led a celibate life.

Newton's secretiveness existed even in his relationships with his friends. When Barrow, who initiated Newton's academic career, asked his assistance in completing a work on optics, Newton readily obliged. However, Barrow's book was out of date before it was finished because Newton did not tell Barrow of his own discoveries in optics. More striking were Newton's lifelong secretly held beliefs opposing the Trinity. When William Whiston, Newton's successor at Cambridge, was dismissed from the university for proffering opinions no different from his own, Newton did not send one word of support. Although Whiston admired Newton, he wrote, "[He is] of the most fearful, cautious and suspicious temper that I ever knew."

Newton was firm and not interested in compromises. Largely because of his opposition to King James II's attempt to include members of the Catholic Church in the administration of the universities, Newton was asked to represent Cambridge in parliament. While in parliament he took no part in any of the great debates of the day. Newton did not talk unless he had something to say. He remained silent except, as someone said, when he asked an usher to close a window.

Newton always did a thorough job. His endurance, persistence, and attention to minute details were remarkable. He attributed much of his success to staying with a problem until it was finished. Examples abound at all levels. Early in his professional career at Cambridge University, he wrote eighteen drafts of a report before accepting one as final, although the last version did not differ much from the others. Six drafts of the scheme for founding the Royal Society were made and seven drafts of his remarks on a chronology.

When Newton devised integral calculus as a young man, he worked out the area of a hyperbola. He was so pleased with his accomplishment, as well he might be, that he carried out one calculation to 52 figures. At that time, and later when he solved Bernoulli's and Leibniz's problems, he followed his routine of attacking the mathematical riddles as soon as he received them. And he stayed with them, omitting food and sleep, until they were solved.

His work was always with him. Several times, while slowly walking away from the college, Newton suddenly stopped, turned about, and dashed back to his room, where he eagerly jotted down the unexpected inspiration.

Newton's absentmindedness undoubtedly was related to preoccupation with his scientific concerns. Even when an old man, he did not change much from the student who forgot to mount his horse and walked several miles home. One evening Dr. Stuckeley was invited to dine with Newton. After waiting an hour, the guest decided to have dinner alone; he ate the whole meal. Newton entering from his study, said, "Give me but leave to take my short dinner and I shall be at your service. I am fatigued and faint." Upon noticing that only a few crumbs remained, he said to Dr. Stuckeley, "See what studious people are! I forgot that I had dined."

An assistant, Humphrey Newton (no relative) worked for Newton while he wrote the *Principia*. The final version of the *Principia* appeared in Humphrey Newton's handwriting. In his letters, Humphrey Newton described Sir Isaac with admiration and affection, if not candor:

> His carriage then was very meek, sedate and humble, never seeming angry, of profound thought, his countenance mild, pleasant and comely. I cannot say I ever saw him laugh but once.... He always kept close to his studies, very rarely went avisiting and had ... few visitors, excepting two or three persons.... I never knew him to take any recreation or pastime either in riding out to take the air, walking, bowling or any other exercise whatever, thinking all hours lost that was not spent in his studies, to which he kept so close that he seldom left his chamber except at term time, when he read in the schools as being Lucasianus professor, where so few went to hear him, and fewer that understood him, that ofttimes he did in a manner, for want of hearers, read to the walls.... When invited to a treat, which was very seldom, he used to return it very handsomely, and with much satisfaction to himself. So intent, so serious upon his studies, that he ate very sparingly, nay, ofttimes he has forgot to eat at all, so that, going into his chamber, I have found his mess untouched, of which, when I have reminded him, he would reply—'Have I?' and then making to the table, would eat a bite or two standing, for I cannot say I ever saw him sit at table by himself.... I cannot say I ever saw him drink either wine, ale or beer, excepting at meals, and then but very sparingly. He very rarely went to dine in the hall, except on some public days, and then if he has not been minded, would go very carelessly, with shoes down at heels, stockings untied, surplice on, and his head scarcely combed....

> Sir Isaac at that time had no pupils.... In his chamber he walked so very much that you might have thought him to be educated at Athens among the Aristotelian sect.... I believe he grudged the short time he spent in eating and sleeping.... He was very charitable, few went empty handed from him....

Though Newton was easy to admire and respect, he was not easy to get along with. Quickly nettled, he needed little provocation to express himself bluntly. Since he did not travel away from the British Isles, most of his personal associations and disagreements were with fellow Englishmen. Newton collided with the able scientists Robert Hooke and John Flamsteed. Hooke studied at Oxford and became the curator of the Royal Society. John Flamsteed was the Astronomer Royal at Greenwich. When Newton published his first paper on light in 1672, Hooke praised him for his valuable experiments and, at the same time, criticized some of his interpretations of the experiments. Newton bluntly rejected Hooke's views and said he would not publish the results of his studies if publication meant controversy. All unpleasantness might have been avoided had Newton at least referred to Hooke's work when he first prepared his own report. Possibly because of Hooke, Newton delayed issuing his *Opticks* until after Hooke died. In 1686 when Newton was working on the *Principia*, Hooke further antagonized him by claiming that he gave Newton the idea of the inverse square law of gravity.

It is easy to side with Newton during the early part of this controversy. When Newton conceived an idea, he wanted priority credit. He also waited for years to make his findings public. Initially, he simply would not acknowledge Hooke just to appease him for a concept he had not used. But later Hooke, despondent and ill, helplessly watched Newton's ascendancy in science, and Newton, callously and self-righteously, persisted in ignoring Hooke's needs and contributions.

Newton's differences with Flamsteed bordered on persecution. Flamsteed, an excellent astronomer, published little, partly because he was so thorough. He was poor and often ill.

Newton depended on Flamsteed's accurate observations for his laws of gravity and planetary motion. Yet, because Flamsteed disliked Halley, Newton's friend, and was quirky, Newton became annoyed with him. This much is clear and understandable. But by using his influence to keep the dedicated and accomplished scientist out of the Royal Society, preventing publication of his life's work, and discontinuing an acknowledgement to him in later editions of the *Principia*, Newton showed the bad side of a determined, single-minded attitude. It is not surprising that Flamsteed said Newton was "insidious, ambitious and excessively covetous of praise and impatient of contradiction."

Newton's friend, the sympathetic physician-philosopher, John Locke, said, "Newton was a difficult man to deal with and a little too apt to raise in himself suspicions where there was no ground."

The more Newton tried to avoid disputes, the more he became involved. He, who wanted no arguments, entered the lists with Leibniz over the origin of the calculus—the most celebrated controversy in the history of science. Without question, Newton was the first to devise and use both differential and integral calculus. For many years, however, he kept the information to himself or made it available only to a few associates. Sometime later, on an independent basis and through a different approach, Leibniz invented the calculus. He and Johann Bernoulli popularized calculus throughout the continent. Leibniz never claimed that Newton copied him but said that he had devised the calculus on his own and made it known to the world. The open dispute between these men and their supporters was not always on a highly ethical plane.

The emotional barrenness of Newton's childhood without a

father, augmented by his mother's leaving him when she remarried, undoubtedly made a lasting mark.

Two serious emotional illnesses occurred, the lesser when Newton was an undergraduate. He suffered a temporary breakdown, details of which are lacking, while observing a comet for many nights without ceasing. He did not sleep or eat for several days before the breakdown. But he recovered rapidly and afterwards forced himself to rest each night.

Just before Newton was 50, he experienced a far more severe episode of nervous agitation which lasted for approximately two years. During the previous five or six years, he had produced an enormous amount of work under a great deal of pressure. For example, when he was 44 he published the *Principia*. At 45 he represented the university in parliament. In the following year Newton suffered a setback. He was not nominated Provost of King's College and felt sensitive about it.

Previously, Newton had little contact with people. His scientific efforts were staggering. For a number of years he had worked two or three times the hours per week that most people do and had already accomplished work that several men might not have accomplished by working together. Newton balked at the total dedication required to complete a project and said that science was dull and barren. He did not take criticism well and hated to deal with personal problems. The disputes over priority and the personality conflicts became impossible for him.

Before the second breakdown, Newton went through a period of being constantly upset and was unable to sleep. He also lost weight. He expressed strong paranoid views in letters to friends. Many believed a psychosis was imminent. Whether or not Newton was confined to the college while he was disturbed is not known. He recovered within a couple of years but felt unhappy and restive at Cambridge. He had to get another position. He and his close friends realized that he could not keep up the pace he had set for himself. At the age of 54, after 35 years at Cambridge University, Newton left for London, without regrets, to become Warden of the Mint. He actively avoided creative work, but the work he had already done in science was all that one could ask.

At the time of his breakdown, Newton wrote to Samuel Pepys and John Locke spontaneously, not in answer to letters from them.

Newton to Locke

[*January 26, 1692*]

Sir,

Being fully convinced that Mr. Montague, upon an old grudge which I thought had been worn out, is false to me, I have done with him, and intend to sit still, unless my Lord Monmouth be still my friend. I have now no prospect of seeing you any more, unless you will be so kind as to repay that visit I made you the last year. If I may hope for this favour, I pray bring my papers with you. Otherwise I desire you would send them by some convenient messenger, when opportunity shall serve. My humble service to my Lady Masham, and to Sir Francis if at Oates.

I am

Your most humble servant,

Is. Newton.

Newton to Locke

[*September 16, 1693*]

Sir,

Being of opinion that you endeavoured to embroil me with women and by other means, I was so much affected with it, as that when one told me you were sickly and would not live, I answered, 'twere better if you were dead. I desire you to forgive me this uncharitableness. For I am now satisfied that what you have done is just, and I beg your pardon for my having hard thoughts of you for it, and for representing that you struck at the root of morality, in a principle you laid down in your book of ideas, and designed to pursue in another book, and that I took you for a Hobbist. I beg your pardon also for saying or thinking that there was a design to sell me an office, or to embroil me.

I am your most humble
And unfortunate servant,
Is. Newton.

Locke to Newton

[October 5, 1693]

Sir,

I have been ever since I first knew you, so entirely and sincerely your friend, and thought you so much mine, that I could not have believed what you tell me of yourself, had I had it from any body else. And though I cannot but be mightily troubled that you should have so many wrong and unjust thoughts of me, yet next to the return of good offices, such as from a sincere good will I have ever done you, I receive your acknowledgement of the contrary as the kindest thing you could have done me, since it gives me hopes that I have not lost a friend I so much valued. After what your letter expresses, I shall not need to say any thing to justify myself to you. I shall always think your own reflection on my carriage both to you and all mankind, will sufficiently do that. Instead of that, give me leave to assure you, that I am more ready to forgive you than you can be to desire it; and I do it so freely and fully, that I wish for nothing more than the opportunity to convince you that I truly love and esteem you; and that I have still the same good will for you as if nothing of this had happened. To confirm this to you more fully, I should be glad to meet you any where, and the rather, because the conclusion of your letter makes me apprehend it would not be wholly useless to you. But whether you think it fit or not, I leave wholly to you. I shall always be ready to serve you to my utmost, in any way you shall like, and shall only need your commands or permission to do it.

My book is going to the press for a second edition; and though I can answer for the design with which I writ it, yet since you have so opportunely given me notice of what you have said of it, I should take it as a favour, if you would point out to me the places that gave occasion to that censure, that by explaining myself better, I may avoid being mistaken by others, or unawares doing the least prejudice to truth or virtue. I am sure you are so much a friend to them both, that were you none to me, I could expect this from you. But I cannot doubt but you would do a great deal more than this for my sake, who after all have all the concern of a friend for you, wish you extremely well, and am without compliment.

[The draft of the letter is endorsed: "J. L. to Is. Newton."]

Newton also wrote Locke on the same day and apparently was already improved.

Newton to Locke

[*October 5, 1693*]

Sir,

The last winter, by sleeping too often by my fire, I got an ill habit of sleeping; and a distemper, which this summer has been epidemical, put me farther out of order, so that when I wrote to you, I had not slept an hour a night for a fortnight together, and for five nights together not a wink. I remember I wrote to you, but what I said of your book I remember not. If you please to send me a transcript of that passage, I will give you an account of it if I can.

I am your most humble servant,

Is. Newton.

Newton to Pepys

[*September 13, 1693*]

Sir,

Some time after Mr. Millington had delivered your message, he pressed me to see you the next time I went to London. I was averse; but upon his pressing consented, before I considered what I did, for I am extremely troubled at the embroilment I am in, and have neither ate nor slept well this twelve-month, nor have my former consistency of mind. I never designed to get any thing by your interest, nor by King James's favour, but am now sensible that I must withdraw from your acquaintance, and see neither you nor the rest of my friends any more, if I may but leave them quietly. I beg your pardon for saying I would see you again, and rest your most humble and most obedient servant,

Is. Newton.

Pepys to Newton

[November 22, 1693]

Sir,

However this comes accompanied to you with a little trouble, yet I cannot but say, that the occasion is welcome to me, in that it gives me an opportunity of telling you that I continue sensible of my obligations to you, most desirous of rendering you service in whatever you shall think me able, and no less afflicted when I hear of your being in town, without knowing how to wait on you till it be too late for me to do it. This said, and with great truth and respect, I go on to tell you that the bearer, Mr. Smith, is one I bear great goodwill to, no less for what I personally know of his general ingenuity, industry, and virtue, than for the general reputation he has in this town, inferior to none, but superior to most, for his mastery in the two points of his profession; namely, fair writing, and arithmetic, so far, principally, as is subservient to accountantship. Now, so it is, that the late project, of which you cannot but have heard, of Mr. Neale, the Groom-Porter's lottery, has almost extinguished for some time, at all places of public conversation in this town, especially among men of numbers, every other talk but what relates to the doctrine of determining between the true proportion of the hazards incident to this or that given chance or lot. On this occasion, it has fallen out that this gentleman is become concerned, more than in jest, to compass a solution that may be relied upon beyond what his modesty will suffer him to think his own alone, or any less than Mr. Newton's, to be, to a question which he takes a journey on purpose to attend you with and prayed my giving him this introduction to you to that purpose, which, not in common friendship only, but as due to his so earnest application after truth, though in a matter of speculation alone, I cannot deny him; and therefore trust you will forgive me in it, and the trouble I desire you to bear, at my instance, of giving him your decision upon it, and the process of your coming at it: wherein I shall esteem myself on his behalf greatly owing to you, and remain,

Honored Sir, your most humble,
And most affectionate and faithful Servant,   S. P.

Einstein

Einstein's requirements for a satisfactory existence were minimal. In college he had little money for food, but that was no problem because his needs were small. Often a slice of apple or plum tart sufficed for supper. His favorite dish was macaroni or spaghetti with cheese and tomatoes. After a meal of macaroni, he invariably remarked, "It couldn't be made any better." He drank tea and coffee but disliked beer and other alcoholic beverages. After meals and occasionally at other times he smoked large, inexpensive cigars which often offended those near him. He smoked until his teeth became discolored and his throat felt sore. After the episode of cardiac distress, he was forced to give up cigars, and he began to smoke a pipe.

Einstein wanted everything around him to be plain. His room was as bare as possible. He shaved with regular soap, not shaving cream. He was not interested in dress and slept without clothes in hot weather. Except for long walks, he did not exercise. He genuinely needed music. Even when playing the violin and piano, he wanted simplicity. His violin bore no prestigious label but was an inexpensive model from Japan. He seldom traveled without his violin in hand.

Einstein enjoyed being on the water and found tranquility in ocean travel and in sailing—a favorite pastime. He liked to be the skipper when he sailed. His boat was reduced to the essentials with no extra gadgets. The wind and the water gave him pleasure; he did not want speed.

Although Einstein had no use for gadgets, he was immensely interested in the principles on which they operated. Einstein did not play chess. He was not interested in competitive events and could see no satisfaction in showing that one person was better than another. To hunt and kill an animal was out of the question; it was repulsive. He had no special interest in art. He read many of the classics but not modern literature.

Einstein did his research either in his private room at home or at the institute, alone or with an associate. He liked to discuss his ideas out loud with his colleagues. At Princeton, Einstein had two adjoining rooms—a small, outer chamber for an assistant and a large, inner one for himself. In practice, however, Einstein reversed the arrangement by using only the small room while his assistant or a visitor occupied the large one. After he derived an equation, he checked and rechecked his work to make sure that each step followed in a rigorous, logical sequence. His self-criticism was brutal. After he had finished and knew that the solution was correct, he would say that if his initial premise were true, then such and such an event "must be so." He never said, "could be so" or "should be so." He was so dedicated to truth that he did not object to being shown his own mistakes. It was the solution of a problem that interested him. He wrote reports about his findings which were concise and to the point, and which omitted unnecessary details. His handwriting, like Newton's, was easy to read. He, too, wrote letters and made notes about his work on used paper.

Einstein's personality consisted of a unique array of admirable traits. Substitute Einstein for Newton in the earlier description of Newton: "Quiet, kind, conscientious, unassuming, independent but not rebellious, he kept to himself and did not have to talk." But these characteristics were not equally balanced in the two men. Other personality factors differed completely.

Einstein possessed wit and humor, together with a sense of the political, social and religious problems of man. His trademark was humility combined with lack of pretense, and he behaved naturally without trying to impress. He had an unusual ability to concentrate. Haste, tension—anything detrimental to concentration—was painful. Throughout his life he had one major interest—physics.

With a fine ear for music, Einstein took violin lessons for two years beginning at the age of six or seven. He stopped taking lessons because he did not like formal instruction and taught himself to play both the violin and piano. His favorite composers were Mozart, Haydn, Bach, Schubert, and Schütz. He did not like modern or popular music, voice, or recordings. He enjoyed playing the piano and improvising in the style of Mozart or Haydn.

Several stories about Einstein's interest in music have been told. While completing high school in Aarau, he learned that the great violinist, Josef Joachim, was to play in a Brahms recital. Einstein carefully prepared himself by practicing for months the sonata to be featured. A high school classmate said of Einstein, "When he began to play his violin the room seemed to broaden out. What fire there was in his playing! I no longer recognized him. He could not help himself."

At a public concert held at a church one evening, Einstein played the first violin part of a composition for several instruments by Bach. With admiration, the second violinist asked Einstein after the performance, "Do you count the beats?" Einstein laughed, "Heavens No! It's in my blood."

There was little shyness when it came to music. Susanne Markwalder, the daughter of the landlady with whom Einstein lived as a college student, told the following story:

> One summer day he was about to fetch his violin and close the balcony door when he heard someone playing one of Mozart's piano sonatas. "Who's the pianist?" he asked. "Do you know her?" I told him that it must be the piano teacher who lived in the attic of a neighbor's house. He hurriedly put his violin under his arm and rushed out without collar or tie. "You can't go like that, Herr Einstein," I cried, but either he did not hear or pretended not to hear me. A moment later the garden gate banged, and it was not long before we heard a violin accompanying the Mozart sonata. On his return, Einstein said with great enthusiasm, "That's a really charming little old lady. I shall often go and play with her." We were to meet a few hours later. It was old Fraülein Wegelin who soon appeared in a black silk dress and asked shyly the name of this extraordinary young man. We pacified her by saying that he was merely a harmless student. She told us what a shock it had given her when the unknown musician rushed into her room and merely said, "Go on playing."

Years later Dr. Janos Plesch was to say to Einstein's playing,

> He was not a very good technical performer but I don't know anyone who exceeded him in fervor and sensibility. He would practice very zealously for his beloved chamber music evenings but it was in this field that he felt the gap between desire and performance most deeply. In a waterside pavilion I had an organ and Einstein often went there on his own and extemporized sometimes for hours on end. When this happened on Saturdays and Sundays there was always a great crowd gathered outside on the river in boats, canoes, yachts, and so forth, listening gratefully to his remarkable performances. It was not mere curiosity that drew them; no one knew that it was Einstein who

was playing. It was the sheer musical enjoyment his playing offered. Not that Einstein was a virtuoso; he was not. . . .

Einstein's sense of humor and easy laughter stood out. He liked to tell jokes, even risqué ones, but did a poor job. About halfway through a story, a glitter appeared in his eyes and a smile on his lips. Before he got the punch line out, he was laughing uncontrollably. This comic situation delighted his listeners. During Einstein's first trip to America with the Chaim Weizmanns, Vera Weizmann said, "Einstein was young, gay, and flirtatious. His wife . . . told me that she did not mind her husband's flirting with me as 'intellectual women did not attract him; out of pity he was attracted to women who did physical work.'"

The physicist, Sommerfeld, also spoke of Einstein's "golden humor." In 1915, at the age of 36, Einstein met the French writer and pacifist, Romain Rolland, in Switzerland, to discuss the possibility of ending the war. Of Einstein, Rolland wrote in his diary, "He is very much alive and fond of laughter. He cannot help giving an amusing twist to the most serious thoughts."

Later Dr. Plesch wrote:

> The gift of laughter has been given him in full measure. There is nothing of the preternaturally solemn professor about him. He can laugh heartily and he does. He enjoys a joke, and he can often see the funny side of situations most people would regard as utterly tragic, and I don't mean utterly tragic for other people, but for himself. I have known him laugh even when a mishap or misfortune has really moved him. . . . he never loses his sense of humor no matter what the situation. . . . He greatly appreciates mother wit and is as delighted as a child with his own witticisms, even when sometimes a biting remark slips from his lips amongst friends. . . . His company is easeful.

Einstein's wit shone under the most adverse personal circumstances. Shortly after graduation and his unsuccessful efforts to get a job, he wrote his friend, Marcel Grossman: "I refuse to lose my sense of humor. God created the donkey and gave him a thick skin. My musical friends here save me from going to pot."

Years later, after he was confined to bed for three months, he wrote to a friend in Switzerland: "I nearly came to grief last year myself but it seems that certain weeds in my innards triumphed."

In 1930 aboard ship to the United States, an artist sketched Einstein who was sitting nearby. Afterwards the artist asked Einstein to sign the sketch. At the bottom of the drawing Einstein wrote: "This fat little pig (*schwein*) is Professor Einstein."

When his small boat capsized and he was being helped out of the water, he remarked, "Make sure this bath is on my record."

In 1920 Einstein answered a request to attend a meeting:

Saying No has never been a strong point with me, but in my present distress I am at last gradually learning the art. Since the flood of newspaper articles I have been so swamped with questions, invitations, challenges that I dream that I am burning in Hell and that the postman is the devil eternally roaring at me, throwing new bundles of letters at my head because I have not yet answered the old ones. In addition to this at home I have my mother who is on her death bed and I have to spend the best part of this "great occasion" in countless meetings and so forth.

In short I am no more than a bundle of poor reflex actions. So I ask merely clemency and compassion. Please pacify Sommerfeld by giving him a true picture of my really unenviable position —glittering misery.

Einstein's humility, naturalness, and humor are evident in the letter written to his non-Jewish Swiss friend, Marcel Grossmann, in 1908 while Einstein was still at the patent office.

Bern, 3 January 1908

Dear Marcel,
  At the risk of your laughing at me, I want to ask your advice in

a practical matter. I would like to apply for a chair at the Institute of Technology in Winterthur (Mathematics and Physics), which probably will become vacant as a friend of mine told me privately.

Don't think that I am suffering from megalomania or that I am moved by dubious passions and ambitions; rather, I have the ardent desire to continue my scientific work under less unfavorable conditions, which I believe you understand. But, you might think, why do I want to grab this particular job? I am doing this because I believe that my chances of obtaining the position are good for the following reasons:

1. I worked there for several months as an auxiliary instructor.

2. I am on friendly terms with one of their teachers.

Now I ask you: how does one go about this? Can I perhaps call on somebody to demonstrate personally the high worth of my commendable self as a teacher and citizen? Who would be the right person to see? Will I make a bad impression (not speaking Swiss-German, my Semitic appearance, etc.)? Would it make sense if I emphasized on this occasion the value of my scientific papers?

Are you pleased with Fiedler's chair? It surely must be more pleasant in those rooms for the poor devils of the Polytechnic than it was for me when I had to make those drawings. Ehrat was with us over Christmas. We spent pleasant days together.

Best regards to clever Eugene, your wife, parents and sisters. And good luck for the next year.

Your old A. Einstein

Friendly greetings from my wife.

Einstein often imbedded his sarcastic wit in a rhyme. When a lady sent Einstein a photograph of himself and asked him to autograph it, he rose to the occasion and wrote, "A thought that sometimes makes me hazy/Am I—or are the others crazy?"

Later, when the Nazis came to power, Einstein resigned from the Prussian Academy because he no longer wanted anything to do with Germany. Max Planck and other friends in the society felt relieved that the resignation came before it was asked of him. The Bavarian Academy of Science then expelled Einstein. After he received an official acknowledgement of receipt of his resignation from the Prussian Academy, he wrote to himself in burning sarcasm, "Thank you for your note so tender, 'Tis typically German like its sender."

In 1947, at the age of 68, Einstein met with scientists at Princeton to discuss control of atomic energy. He wrote the following for himself.

Resolution

We American Scientists after three days of careful consideration have come to the following conclusions. We do not know:

(a)   What to believe

(b)   What to wish for

(c)   What to say

(d)   What to do.

Appendix

On the basis of an open letter signed by Russian scientists you may construct a parallel resolution for them. After careful consideration and after due consultation with our government we do not know:

(a)   What not to believe

(b)   What not to wish for

(c)   What not to say

(d)   What not to do.

Einstein's good nature and sense of humor never left him. A few weeks before he died he wrote to his old friends, Niels Bohr in Denmark and Queen Elizabeth of Belgium. Trying to elicit Bohr's support for a statement by Bertrand Russell on atomic weapons, Einstein began: "Don't frown like that! This has nothing to do with our old controversy on physics but rather concerns a matter on which we are in complete agreement."

To the Queen he commented on the story of the moon written by the 18th century physicist, Lichtenberg:

Question: Which is more useful, the sun or the moon?

Answer: The moon of course; it shines when it is quite dark while the sun shines only when it is light anyhow.

Einstein was not a practical jokester or a clown who had to be funny. His interests lay in nature and in mankind, and his sense of humor, though excellent, was incidental. His many writings on political and social issues, beautiful examples of clear, concise thinking, seldom contained humor.

Einstein was an inborn pacifist. As a child, he feared and disliked men in uniform. He objected to the military-like method of teaching and maintaining discipline in the German primary and secondary schools. He was suspicious of authority and had an aversion to the herd instinct. Seeing men march to band music disturbed him. "When a person can march with pleasure in the ranks in step to a piece of music, I have the greatest contempt for him. He has only been given his big brain by mistake; his spinal cord would have amply sufficed him." Because he was so independent in thought and had to evaluate each problem as it arose, he could not see how anyone could belong wholeheartedly to a political party.

Man's cruelty to his fellow man repelled Einstein. At the beginning of the first World War, Einstein wrote two letters to Paul Ehrenfest on this point. Here are some excerpts:

Europe in her insanity has started something unbelievable. In such times one realizes to what a sad species of animal one belongs. I quietly pursue my peaceful studies and contemplations and feel only pity and disgust. . . . The international catastrophe has imposed a heavy burden upon me as an internationalist. In living through this "great epoch," it is difficult to reconcile oneself to the fact that one belongs to that idiotic, rotten species which boasts of its freedom of will.

After the war, when much hostility was directed towards Einstein for being a pacifist and a Jew, he wrote to a friend in China in 1921: "I shudder when I think of all that has happened in this world since last we met, and of what may yet await us. It is almost cheering to think that someday it will be all over, one's own life as well."

Einstein had no interest in formal affairs. "Feeding time at the zoo" was his description of banquets. Yet he allowed himself to be used "for table decoration" in situations where he could be helpful. He felt that he should put his fame into service for mankind. He never understood why he was so famous and received so much attention. He described his dilemmas in entries to his diary in December 1930, when he traveled from England to America.

The excessive and pretentious attention makes one uncomfortable. I feel like an indirect exploiter of labor. . . . Every member of the crew behaves with such dignity and simplicity that one feels odd about one's own unpolished manners. . . . Worse than the most fanciful anticipation. Just off Long Island hordes of reporters swarmed aboard. . . . The passengers are becoming more and more annoying. There is no end to the business of taking photographs. . . . Everyone has to have his picture taken with me. The autograph business for the benefit of charity is flourishing. They make a dreadful fuss over me. Where will it all end?

Many years later, several weeks after his 75th birthday, he wrote to Queen Elizabeth in Belgium:

> Once again you have thought of me in such a friendly way on this strange occasion. Actually, unless an individual has already departed, he automatically turns 75 without any particular effort. But, having reached that stage, he feels bewildered and awkward since he is quite incapable of proving himself worthy of the many demonstrations of affection—especially when he has, through no will of his own, become a kind of legend in his own lifetime. All manner of fable is being attached to his personality, and there is no end to the number of ingeniously devised tales.

And in his last letter to the Queen, a year later on his 76th birthday and a few weeks before he died:

> I must confess that the exaggerated esteem in which my lifework is held makes me feel very ill at ease. I feel compelled to think of myself as an involuntary swindler. If one attempts to do anything about this, one succeeds only in making matters worse.

Einstein maintained that he "never belonged wholeheartedly to a country, a state, nor to a circle of friends nor even to my own family," but there is evidence to the contrary. He had numerous loyal friends, and people who met him remained impressed by his bright and simple qualities. He was very close to his immediate family. As a high school student, he was so lonesome for his family when they left for Italy that within a few months he quit school to join them. When Einstein was 23, his father died. He greatly admired his father and felt real grief upon his death. He wondered why he should be allowed to live when a human being as wonderful as his father had to die.

Perhaps the most impressive of Einstein's characteristics was the lasting zeal with which he sought the laws of nature. Good research is nearly always the result of extremely demanding effort, and it is difficult to continue such research on a long term basis. Einstein was the great exception. He should have won an Olympic record for persistence. At 15 he knew that he wanted to study the physical world, and he kept to his objective for 60 years. As he lay near death, he went over some formulas and complained that he wished he knew more mathematics. No matter what extra project engaged him, he always wanted to get back to physics. At 63 Einstein wrote to a friend:

> In my work I am more fanatical than ever and I really entertain the hope that I have solved my own problems of the unity of the physical world. I have to function as a saint for the Jews and bestow my blessings on all the Gentiles so for thinking and working I have virtually to steal the time like a professional thief.

When Einstein received a compass from his father at the age of four or five, he wondered how it worked and never stopped wondering. He had the determination, persistence, and talent to stay with the problem. Einstein acted like a Talmudic scholar. Instead of devoting a lifetime to religion, ethics and legal problems, however, he made a lifelong study of nature.

Einstein had no overt emotional problems. His first wife, younger son and some members of his wife's family experienced psychiatric difficulties. At times his first wife—withdrawn, depressed and disorganized—avoided meeting people. The exact diagnosis of her illness is not known. Why they were divorced is not clear. His second marriage, to a divorced first cousin with two daughters, was successful.

Einstein was fond of both his sons, Hans Albert and Eduard. The older one became a professor of engineering at the University of California. Eduard was interested in medicine, but he developed schizophrenia at the age of 21 and could not continue his studies. He lived in Switzerland, occasionally was hospitalized, and died of a stroke at the age of 55.

Einstein did his best to keep personal affairs private. "I don't want anyone walking through my life," was a stock comment.

Comparison

In comparing the personalities and habits of Newton and Einstein, one must keep in mind that Newton underwent a striking change after his nervous breakdown at 50. For the moment let us limit the comparison to the time before then. Overall a certain uniformity marked the simple way in which they lived. Neither was interested in material sustenance — food and drink — or in dress. Both slept without clothes. They did not like sports and avoided competitive physical activity. Neither condoned hunting. Both abhorred cruelty and violence. They were men of strict principles and high personal integrity. They were not great readers and had no special interest in art.

Success came to both men in the same way. Their efforts were directed towards solving problems of their own choosing. They did not compete with anyone, strive for jobs or promotions, or seek material gain from their work.

Newton possessed outstanding physical sensibilities together with manual dexterity. He liked to make things with his hands and to carry out experiments. Einstein, with a good ear for music, was an enthusiastic violinist and pianist. He smoked cigars and a pipe, but Newton did not smoke at all. Only Einstein liked to sail. Newton paced the floor in his room; Einstein went for long walks.

Both were kind, humble, modest, and religious men who disliked publicity. They were loners who worked constantly, following patterns set early in life. Although each man worked alone, there was a difference. Newton was totally alone. He communicated his thoughts to no one, at least not until he had completed something, and kept many of his writings secret. Although compulsive in writing reports of his findings for himself, he had to be coaxed into making the information generally available. He was shy, silent, suspicious, and sensitive. Einstein liked to talk things out with one or two friends. He never feared expressing his thoughts. Usually he had an assistant to help with calculations. Only when his work was at a highly critical state did he have to be completely alone. Einstein was not suspicious or secretive but direct and straightforward.

Newton, always serious, did not joke. "I cannot say I ever saw him laugh but once [in five years]." Einstein often joked about himself. "The gift of laughter has been given to him in full measure."

Both men had a fantastic ability to concentrate. Einstein liked to sit quietly and think. When a cleaning woman entered his room and saw him wide-eyed and motionless in his chair, she was startled and reported to Einstein's secretary that he was not well. Newton carried this talent further. He could work on a problem continuously, in the most precise sense, skipping sleep and meals for more than 24 hours at a stretch. In fact he carried his tenacity to the point of temporary psychosis. After Newton realized that work without sleep produced emotional difficulties, he made an effort to sleep every night.

Newton and Einstein were doers more than teachers. Newton did not have one successful student of mathematics or physics. It is true that he helped at least four young, qualified mathematicians, but he did not train them. Einstein liked teaching, but he usually worked alone or with an assistant. Over the years, he had the good fortune to associate with many capable people, but rarely did he have a student working for a graduate degree. One, Otto Stern, went on to win a Nobel Prize in physics.

Both men worked with unbelievable persistence. Einstein took time from his responsibilities at the patent office and from family affairs to be alone with his thoughts about the natural world. All his life distractions plagued him, many of great importance; yet he always returned to physics. His sixty or more years of devotion to science may be a record.

Newton, completely isolated, had no distractions. After many years of labor, he felt that he had to give up creative work in science. He must have known that he could not continue. He tried to secure a post away from the scientific milieu but was unsuccessful. A nervous breakdown followed. When he recovered, his friends obtained a position at the mint for him. He still could solve the most difficult problems in mathematics, and he edited many of his writings. But he was a different man. He dressed properly, put on weight, interested himself in social standing, and devoted time to discovering his family tree. Happy to be knighted and to preside over the Royal Society for many years, he easily became as Lord Keynes said, "the Sage and Monarch of the Age of Reason." In this period Frances Atterbury found that Newton "had something rather languid in his look and manner." He spoke very little in company. And from Newton, "I have not the former consistency of mind."

Under no circumstances should one exaggerate the unattractive aspects of Newton's personality—his inclination to be secretive and irritable. It is true that in a few instances he behaved poorly. But, like Einstein, he had a deep-seated sense of justice and was devoted to the spirit of freedom. Newton wanted to be left alone and was content not to talk about his work in science or theology. He did not originate arguments. People who knew of his superb achievements urged him to make the information public. Later, when anyone questioned his findings, Newton over-reacted. Yet he often accepted with good grace and appreciation the correction of actual errors. It is even possible that Newton's pique resulted from hyperthyroidism.

Einstein's personality changed little. He felt deeply discouraged by man's cruelty. The problems of war and the atomic bomb weighed heavily. He became a lonely man, but he stayed with physics. He never wanted material possessions; and his fame embarrassed him.

Religion

Einstein and Newton considered themselves religious. Each believed that his religious spirit was a motivating factor in his efforts to formulate some of the basic laws of nature. However, there has been much confusion about their attitudes. Newton's voluminous writings in theology were not studied carefully until after 1930, and the objectivity of earlier evaluations is questionable. It seems that his manuscripts were read with predetermined interpretation or to support a cause. Einstein, who clearly set forth his opinions on religion and on Jewish problems, was often misinterpreted by even well-intentioned scholars.

Newton

Theology was not a part-time hobby for Newton but a subject he studied actively. As in mathematics and physics, he prepared himself well and kept an independent outlook. Religious pursuits demanded less than science, and he stayed with them all his life. Nevertheless, Newton accomplished the bulk of his theological work during the period of his creativity in mathematics and physics at Cambridge and not afterwards.

Newton was raised in a religious environment. The uncle with whom he lived and his stepfather were in holy orders. Two ministers of the church that he attended while boarding with the Clark family in Grantham were ultimately discharged for nonconformity. Thus, at an early age, Newton was made aware of both theological subtleties and the dangers of dissension.

Newton, well-schooled in Latin and knowing Greek and Hebrew, had a sound basis for theological study. He wrote over a million words, more than 17 volumes, on a variety of subjects that included "Chronology, Apocalyptic Literature, Church History, Prophecy, Ecclesiastical Polity, the Nature and Content of Religion, the Relation of Jews and Christians, Roman Catholicism, the Sibylline Oracles, Solomon's Temple, Trinitarianism and New Testament Textual Criticism." In addition he made ". . . copious extracts from the Bible, patristic literature and early ecclesiastical history. . . ." His library contained numerous books on theological subjects which he discussed with Archbishop Tenison, Henry More, John Locke, and others. Newton felt more in accord with Locke, a Unitarian.

Archbishop Tenison said to Newton, "You know more about divinity than all of us put together." John Locke wrote, "Mr. Newton is a very valuable man, not only for his wonderful skill in mathematics, but in divinity too, and his great knowledge of the Scriptures, wherein I know few his equals. . . ." Shortly after Newton died, his friend, the mathematician, John Craig, wrote:

This I know that he was much more solicitious in his inquiries into Religion than into [science]. . . . Sir Isaac Newton, to make his inquiries into the Christian religion more successful, had read the ancient writers and ecclesiastical historians with great exactness, and had drawn up in writing great collections out of both and to show how earnest he was in religion, he had written a long explication of remarkable parts of the Old and New Testaments while his understanding was in its greatest perfection lest the infidels might pretend that his applying himself to the study of religion was the effect of dotage. That he would not publish these writings in his own time, because they showed that his thoughts were sometimes different from those which are commonly received, which would engage him in dispute; and this was a thing which he avoided as much as possible. . . .

For 200 years nonobjective interpreters muddled the picture of Newton's religious views. In 1934, however, the physicist, Louis Trenchard More, tried to clarify Newton's writings and presented him as a strong Protestant. In an excellent book on Newton's theological work, Dr. H. McLachlin wrote in 1950, "It is certain that Newton's posthumous works were intended to uphold Protestantism and to combat the claims of the Roman church. This zeal is confirmed by his numerous manuscripts on scripture, church history and Christian doctrine." In 1960 the mathematician, H. D. Anthony, referred to ". . . that personal loyalty to the Protestant cause so characteristic of Newton the man and so vividly portrayed from time to time in his theological writings." But a different aspect of Newton's religious beliefs were brought to light by Lord Keynes who thoroughly studied his personality and collected and evaluated many of his religious writings. In 1946 Lord Keynes gave a large collection of Newton's works to King's College at Cambridge. Before that time Lord Keynes had written:

Very early in life Newton abandoned orthodox belief in the Trinity. He was a Judaic Monotheist of the School of Maimonides. He arrived at this conclusion not on so-to-speak rational or skeptical grounds but entirely on the interpretation of ancient authority. He was persuaded that the revealed documents gave no support to the Trinitarian doctrines which were due to late falsifications. The revealed God was one God. But this was a dreadful secret which Newton was at desperate pains to conceal all his life. It was the reason why he refused Holy Orders and therefore had to obtain a special dispensation to hold his Fellowship and Lucasian Chair and could not be made Master of Trinity College. In the main, the secret died with him.

On the basis of his exegesis of the Bible, Newton assigned the Jews a place in antiquity that predated the Egyptians, Greeks, Romans, Chinese and other competitors for the honor of being the oldest nation. "Newton too was defending Jewish antiquities against Egyptian falsifiers and maligners," wrote the historian, F. E. Manuel. ". . . the names of hundreds of Egyptian kings on dynastic lists were merely priestly fabrications. . . . Whatever originally induced Newton to write on chronology, on a common sense level the final system appeared as a eulogy of Israel. And the further he ploughed through the vast mass of historical data, the more supporting evidence he accumulated for his central proposition that the Hebrews were the most ancient civilized people, a truth which he had to proclaim. . . . Israel was exalted as the chosen people of God not only for the propagation of the truth about religion, but also for the invention of the first arts and sciences; and all other ancient peoples were mere imitators of the Hebrews."

Einstein

Although Einstein's parents were not formally religious, and he was not called to the Torah as a Bar Mitzvah at age 13, they joined a synagogue in Munich and attended its social functions.

Einstein went to a Catholic elementary school where he was either the only Jewish boy or one of a very few Jews. He experienced little or no difficulty and occasionally helped some of his fellow students answer questions on their assignments in religion. For a brief period, perhaps a year, at about the age of 11, Einstein was challenged by Judaism. By 12 he developed a strong interest in reading books on science and his views changed. ". . . I soon reached the conviction that much in the stories of the Bible could not be true. The consequence was a positively fanatic freethinking coupled with the impression that youth is intentionally being deceived by the state through lies; it was a crushing impression. Suspicion against every kind of authority grew out of this experience, a skeptical attitude towards the convictions which were alive in any specific social environment—an attitude which has never again left me, even though later on, because of a better insight into the causal connections, it lost some of its original poignancy." The girl Einstein met in college, who became his first wife, was Greek Orthodox. Their two sons were baptized in the mother's faith, but they did not maintain their religious affiliations.

When Einstein was 50, and after he published his first papers on the unified field theory, he became the center of a religious controversy. In New York City, a Presbyterian and a Methodist minister praised Einstein for his monumental contributions. However, a cardinal in Boston labeled Einstein an atheist. All this led a rabbi in New York to cable Einstein, "Do you believe in God? Prepaid reply fifty words." Einstein replied immediately and did not use all fifty words. "I believe in Spinoza's God who reveals himself in the harmony of all that exists, not in a God who concerns himself with the fate and actions of man." On another occasion Einstein said:

The cosmic religious experience is the strongest and noblest mainspring of scientific research. My religion consists of a humble admiration of the illimitable superior spirit who reveals himself in the slight details we are able to perceive with our frail and feeble minds. That deeply emotional conviction of the presence of a superior reasoning power which is revealed in the incomprehensible universe forms my idea of God.

A good idea of the importance of religion to Einstein is evident from a discussion he had at the age of 61 with the elderly Swiss theologian, Adolf Keller. They spoke in Princeton about freedom of the human spirit. Einstein, impassioned, criticized Germany for renouncing scientific as well as other freedoms under Hitler and for prostituting herself to violence. Einstein told Keller, "I had always hoped that the German universities would have led the struggle for freedom. I was mistaken. But even if the universities failed, the churches, at least, struggled for this freedom, both the Catholic and the Protestant. This much as a Jew I must recognize, and the struggle must not be forgotten."

Again he emphasized the significance of religion when, in his autobiography at age 67, he introduced the subject early— in the second paragraph. Einstein repeatedly referred to God. Jobless, he joked about himself to Marcel Grossmann, "Fortunately God gave the donkey a thick skin." More important were two profound statements that arose out of a basic religious impulse: "God does not play dice with the universe," and "God is subtle but not malicious."

It is not surprising that the highly abstract nature of Einstein's studies led some people to suspect his attitude toward religion. Physicist Louis Trenchard More wrote:

It is a matter of the deepest regret that Professor Einstein, after his efficient service in extending Newton's ideas of the relativity of our knowledge, should, with his followers, have then plunged into a peculiarly aggravated case of propounding a positive and absolute system of space, time and energy. They have, in essence, thrown science, which had emerged from the Renaissance into a sane and powerful method, back into the spirit of the Middle Ages. If they succeed, our conception of the objective world will be as dogmatic, and as foreign, to our common sense perceptions as were the cosmic ideas of the monks. They created a world founded on a presupposed divine revelation, and we are creating another with no more substantiality than the mathematical symbols and formulae. . . . His [Newton's] scientific work has been built upon as a basis for the attacks on the Christian religion by such scientists as can recognize no phenomena and no laws except those of matter, space and time.

More also referred to Newton's possessing a "restraining balance [that] prevented his imagination from sweeping him into the scientific mysticism which has so dominated the minds of Professor Einstein and his school." But Einstein saw no conflict between science and religion. Here are excerpts from his writings at 60 and 62.

The highest principles for our aspirations and judgments are given to us in the Jewish-Christian religious tradition. It is a very high goal which, with our weak powers, we can reach only very inadequately, but which gives a sure foundation to our aspirations and valuations. If one were to take that goal out of its religious form and look merely at its purely human side, one might state it perhaps thus: free and responsible development of the individual, so that he may place his powers freely and gladly in the service of all mankind. There is no room in this for the divinization of a nation, of a class, let alone of an individual.

If one holds these high principles clearly before one's eyes, and compares them with the life and spirit of our times, then it appears glaringly that civilized mankind finds itself at present in grave danger. In the totalitarian states it is the rulers themselves who strive actually to destroy that spirit of humanity. In less threatened parts it is nationalism and intolerance, as well as the oppression of the individuals by economic means, which threaten to choke these most precious traditions.

It would not be difficult to come to an agreement as to what we mean by science. Science is the century-old endeavor to bring together by means of systematic thought the perceptible phenomena of this world into as thorough-going an association as possible. To put it boldly, it is the attempt at the posterior reconstruction of existence by the process of conceptualization. But when asking myself what religion is I cannot think of the answer so easily. And even after finding an answer which may satisfy me at this particular moment I still remain convinced that I can never under any circumstances bring together, even to a slight extent, all those who have given this question serious consideration.

At first, then instead of asking what religion is I should prefer to ask what characterizes the aspirations of a person who gives me the impression of being religious: A person who is religiously enlightened appears to me to be one who has, to the best of his ability, liberated himself from the fetters of his selfish desires and is pre-occupied with thoughts, feelings, and aspirations to which he clings because of their super-personal value. It seems to me that what is important is the force of this superpersonal content and the depth of the conviction concerning its overpowering meaningfulness, regardless of whether any attempt is made to unite this content with a divine Being, for otherwise it would not be possible to count Buddha and Spinoza as religious personalities. Accordingly, a religious person is devout in the sense that he has no doubt of the significance and loftiness of those super-personal objects and goals which neither require nor are capable of rational foundation. They exist with the same necessity and matter-of-factness as he himself. In this sense religion is the age-old endeavor of mankind to become clearly and completely conscious of these values and goals and constantly to strengthen and extend their effect. If one conceives of religion and science according to these definitions then a conflict between them appears impossible. For science can only ascertain what *is*, but not what *should be*, and outside of its domain value judgments of all kinds remain necessary. Religion, on the other hand, deals only with evaluations of human thought and action: it cannot justifiably speak of facts and relationships between facts. According to this interpretation the well-known conflicts between religion and science in the past must all be ascribed to a misapprehension of the situation which has been described.

For example, a conflict arises when a religious community insists on the absolute truthfulness of all statements recorded in the Bible. This means an intervention on the part of religion into the sphere of science; this is where the struggle of the Church against the doctrines of Galileo and Darwin belongs. On the other hand, representatives of science have often made an attempt to arrive at fundamental judgments with respect to values and ends on the basis of scientific method, and in this way have set themselves in opposition to religion. These conflicts have all sprung from fatal errors.

Now, even though the realms of religion and science in themselves are clearly marked off from each other, nevertheless there exist between the two strong reciprocal relationships and dependencies. Though religion may be that which determines the goal, it has, nevertheless, learned from science, in the broadest sense, what means will contribute to the attainment of the goals it has set up. But science can only be created by those who are thoroughly imbued with the aspiration towards truth and understanding. This source of feeling, however, springs from the sphere of religion. To this there also belongs the faith in the possibility that the regulations valid for the world of existence are rational, that is, comprehensible to reason. I cannot conceive of a genuine scientist without that profound faith. The situation may be expressed by an image: science without religion is lame, religion without science is blind.

More than one friend insisted that Einstein was the most religious person he had known. The ancient Hebrews originated the concept of a single God. Einstein followed their path and devoted his life to finding a unified concept of the physical world. His dedication to science paralleled the Talmudic scholar's quest for an understanding of God's will. I proposed the analogy to the mathematician, Cornelius Lanczos, a former assistant of Einstein and also a religious scholar. He answered, "Einstein was more than a Talmudic scholar. His accomplishments make him one of the Prophets."

Although nationality and religion can be two entirely separate subjects, Einstein's Jewishness deserves comment. Some time ago one biographer stated erroneously that Einstein went through a period in which he broke away from the Jewish community. Later writers repeated the statement. Yet nothing could be farther from the truth. On this very point Einstein remarked, "I cannot be made responsible for what other people write about me. I was entirely aware of my Jewish background though I realized its significance only in later years. At that time I would not have even understood what it meant to leave Judiasm."

It is possible that the misinterpretation arose in the following way. In official documents requesting religious affiliation, Einstein usually wrote *Dissident*, because he did not belong to any religious organization. This procedure was accepted in Germany and Switzerland. In Catholic Austria and Hungary, however, where a statement of religion or nationality at birth was required, he always wrote *Israëlitisch*. In Berlin he joined the Jewish community. Einstein's relationship with the Jewish people was his strongest human bond. He had little sympathy for the assimilated Jew. No other scientist gave as much support to the Jewish people as Einstein.

Comparison

Einstein's and Newton's strong desire to understand nature was associated with their deeply religious attitudes. Initially, Newton was a firm Protestant. Later, in his independent way, and after careful evaluation of theological works, he added some aspects of Judaism and Unitarianism. Einstein closely identified himself with the Jewish people. He did not believe in a personal God but followed the religious views of Spinoza. Newton probably spent as much time in theology as in science. His lifelong interest in religion resulted in an enormous written output. Einstein combined science with religion and subtly extended the idea of one God into his unified concept of the physical world. Both physicists supported the Jewish people: Einstein in their problems of modern times, Newton in their accomplishments during antiquity.

9

Medical Friends

Newton and Einstein, intensely interested in nature, were not keen on biology—Einstein even less than Newton. As youths they required little help from physicians for problems of personal health. However, they depended on medical people for their early development in science. Each had physicians as close personal friends.

Newton

Dr. Clark, the physician who taught at King's School in Grantham, was responsible for Newton's early education in mathematics. Dr. Clark was educated at Cambridge and may have played a part in Newton's decision to go there.

Four physicians—Locke, Pemberton, Meade, and Stuckeley—helped Newton greatly. Most important was John Locke, a double star of medicine and philosophy, ten years older than

Newton and, like him, a bachelor. They first met in London when Newton, at the age of 46, represented the University of Cambridge as a member of the House of Commons. An enduring friendship based on mutual esteem and common interests developed. No other relationship during the year in London was as significant. Through this physician, Newton met people active in the intellectual and political life of England, among whom was Samuel Pepys. Because Locke was interested in the *Principia*, but could not follow its complicated mathematics, Newton prepared for him a short paper containing simplified versions of some of the proofs.

Locke's strong interest in theology also influenced Newton. They discussed, among other subjects, the Trinity and the prophecies. Both favored Unitarianism. Eighteenth century Unitarians rejected the doctrine of the Trinity as well as Calvinist doctrines that emphasized human sinfulness. Newton devoted much time to religious matters and gave Locke many of his theological writings for review and comment. Locke conscientiously tried to obtain a government post for Newton. The two men continued a close friendship until Locke died in 1704.

Another medical man, Dr. Henry Pemberton, had an opportunity to read the *Principia* while studying medicine on the continent. Mathematics and the natural sciences interested him as much as medicine, and he was one of the few people who could follow the *Principia*. Pemberton solved a problem proposed by Leibniz to test the English mathematicians, and he cleverly disproved a claim put forth to overthrow Newton's law of gravity. Newton was so impressed by Pemberton that he asked him to edit the third edition of the *Principia*. The final edition appeared early in 1726, and Newton paid Pemberton 200 guineas for his help. Of their relationship, Pemberton said,

"Neither his extreme great age nor his universal reputation had rendered him stiff in opinion or in any degree elated. Of this I had occasion to have almost daily experience."

After Newton became master of the mint, he met Dr. Richard Meade, a physician who remained a close personal friend and who cared for Newton in the last years of his life.

In 1718, while Newton presided over the Royal Society, Dr. Meade recommended Dr. William Stuckeley, a London physician, for membership as a Fellow. Although Dr. Stuckeley was 45 years younger than Newton, they became good friends. In 1726, a year before Newton died, Dr. Stuckeley moved to Grantham where Newton had gone to school as a boy. For many years he collected biographical information on Newton from the scientist's personal acquaintances. It is largely from his writings that we know about Newton's early life.

Einstein

Physicians played an important part in Newton's career and an even greater role in Einstein's. In the fall of 1955, a few months after Einstein's death, the Albert Einstein College of Medicine opened. When members of Yeshiva University told Einstein, at the age of 74, that they wanted to name their new medical school for him, he felt honored. Einstein, who had received unusual assistance from medical men and who also had enjoyed lifelong personal friendships with them, was able to give something the physicians really wanted—a name symbolic of intellectual achievement for a medical school.

The medical student, Max Talmey, introduced Einstein to science, mathematics, and philosophy. He guided the boy when he disliked his work at school and was considered a poor student by many of his teachers. Although Talmey did not impart ability or initiative to Einstein, he may have stimulated his capacity for self-teaching. It is also of interest that Einstein retained a rigorous philosophical basis for his work in physics.

His fortunate association with Talmey, as well as the example set by his parents who invited Talmey and other foreign students to their house, may explain part of a curious trait seen later in Einstein—one not common to the intellectual Jews of Germany at that time. Einstein was always prepared to help Jewish students from Eastern Europe in any way possible. Some became his assistants. The difficulty experienced by these students in getting a college education led Einstein to champion a Hebrew University in Palestine and subsequently the Zionist cause. Associating with Talmey also may have encouraged Einstein's pronounced antinationalistic beliefs. Max Talmey and later, Marcel Grossmann, Einstein's college classmate, undoubtedly were the two most important people outside the family who helped Albert Einstein.

When Einstein at 15 decided to quit school in Munich and join his parents in Milan, help came to him from the family's physician in the form of a letter to the school officials. The doctor stated that, for emotional reasons, the boy should be with his family in Italy.

The next significant relationship with a medical man began when Einstein worked at the patent office. Dr. Heinrich Zangger, a Swiss physician interested in physics and mathematics who had worked with Marie Curie, was professor of legal medicine at Zurich University. In 1902 one of Dr. Zangger's research projects required the use of more mathematics than he knew. He asked Professor Laurel Stodola in Zurich for assistance and was told, "Talk to Einstein. He will be able to help you." Zangger went to Berne where Einstein had just taken the job at the patent office. Einstein found a quick solution for the problem and acquired a lifelong friend. Zangger immediately recognized Einstein's genius and began a steady effort to get him a position in theoretical physics. In 1909 Zangger succeeded. Zurich University gave Einstein his first academic post—associate professor of theoretical physics. Later the two men worked together for pacifist causes during the first World War. Dr. Zangger helped Einstein with the personal domestic problems in Zurich that preceded and followed his divorce.

In 1905 Einstein completed his PhD thesis. The man responsible for accepting his work was Dr. Alfred Kleiner, director of the physics institute at Zurich University. Dr. Kleiner was a physician-turned-physicist. He, together with Dr. Zangger, succeeded in getting Einstein the faculty position at Zurich University. Einstein was able to leave the patent office and devote full time to his work in theoretical physics.

Following sojourns in Prague and then in Zurich, Einstein became a professor at the Kaiser Wilhelm Institute in Berlin. Shortly after he arrived in the German capital, World War I began. Several weeks later, in October 1914, a group of 93 Germans prominent in the arts and sciences signed a manifesto supporting their country's violation of Belgium's neutrality and denying any wrong doings by German soldiers. Within a few days, Dr. George Friedrich Nicolai, a physician and ardent pacifist, prepared a blunt challenge to the manifesto. Dr. Nicolai held a chair in physiology and carried out research in cardiology. Only Einstein and two others signed his rebuttal to the manifesto which became the first public document to bear Einstein's signature written at the age of 35 in 1914.

In Berlin Einstein was friendly with several physicians including three in internal medicine: Rudolph Ehrmann, Hans Mühsam, and Janos Plesch; a surgeon, Moritz Katzenstein; a radiologist, Gustav Bucky; and a psychiatrist, Otto Juliusburger. Dr. Ehrmann, a specialist in gastroenterology, became Einstein's personal physician. Einstein often took long walks through the woods outside Berlin with either Dr. Ehrmann or Dr. Mühsam. For more than ten years, Einstein and Katzenstein sailed together when they were free during the summer. Dr. Bucky was physician to Einstein's two stepdaughters. Einstein consulted Dr. Juliusburger about a member of the family who had emotional problems. The physicist and psychiatrist became good personal friends.

After the Nazis assumed power, Einstein and his medical friends left Germany. He corresponded with Mühsam in Israel and Plesch in England. In the United States, contacts with Ehrmann, Bucky, and Juliusburger continued. Dr. Bucky was an inventor as well as a radiologist, and Einstein liked helping with his inventions. At the age of 73, Einstein appeared in court as an expert witness to assist Dr. Bucky who had brought a suit for patent infringement against a large company. The Einstein and Bucky families often vacationed together in New York or Connecticut.

In 1921 Einstein came to the United States with Dr. Chaim Weizmann, chemist and leader of the Zionist movement, to raise funds for a Hebrew university to be built in Jerusalem. Einstein gave special thanks to American physicians who were largely responsible for making their venture a success.

On a visit to the Orient in 1922, while aboard a Japanese steamer, Einstein developed abdominal pain. A fellow passenger, Dr. Hayasi Miyake, helped make him comfortable. Before the end of World War II, Dr. Miyake, almost 80, and his wife were killed in an American air raid. Later Einstein sent an epitaph that was chiseled into the couple's tombstone.

Here lie Dr. Hayasi Miyake and wife, Miko Miyake. They labored together for the welfare of man and departed together, victims of human folly.

Respect for the medical profession was evident in a letter Einstein wrote in 1930 to an Arab about how the Jews and Arabs could live together peacefully. Einstein suggested that the areas of conflict be overseen by eight responsible citizens— one Jewish and one Arabian physician, lawyer, labor representative, and religious leader. Perhaps it was not accidental that Einstein listed the physician first. His advice on the Arab-Jewish problem is still good.

Einstein and Sigmund Freud, 21 years his senior, met personally at least twice and on special occasions exchanged letters. In 1929 Freud wrote to a friend about Einstein, "You have strikingly isolated the real, true, almost naive elements that make up the greatness of this rare man—his freedom from countless human foibles." At the suggestion of the League of Nations, Einstein addressed an open letter to Freud on the cause and prevention of war. Within a few months, the 74-year-old Freud returned an essay. The analyses by these two giants of the all important problem of war are classics that deserve to be published in any book about the life of either man. They are included in Appendix A of this volume.

In 1931 on a visit to California, Einstein was treated for a minor illness by Dr. Gabriel Segall. As had happened many times before, the physician and Einstein developed a lifelong friendship. Dr. Guy K. Dean of Princeton took care of Einstein from 1946 until he died. Sometimes Helen Dukas or Ein-

stein's stepdaughter, Margot, requested that Dr. Dean make a
house call late in the evening because Einstein was having
severe abdominal or back pain related to the aortic aneurysm.
Dr. Dean instructed the family to phone anytime he was needed, but Einstein insisted that the physician be called only during
daytime hours. When Dr. Dean arrived, Einstein would be upset and state that the pain was his own and not Helen Dukas',
Margot's, or the physician's. But within a few minutes, the at-
mosphere once more would become peaceful. An injection of
demerol would control the pain. In 1947 Dr. Rudolf Nissen
performed an abdominal operation on Einstein. Again the physician and patient developed close ties.

Comparison

In Clark and Talmey, Newton and Einstein had medical men
as their first teachers of mathematics. More than once, they
depended on physicians for assistance in problems unrelated
to medicine. Newton, working in theology, leaned heavily on
John Locke. Henry Pemberton helped in the third edition of
the *Principia*, and Dr. William Stuckeley became Newton's
first biographer.

Physicians played key roles in securing Einstein's first academic position—Alfred Kleiner and Heinrich Zangger; in his
first signing a public document—George Nicolai; and in pro-
viding funds for the Hebrew University. The open letters exchanged with Sigmund Freud made a joint contribution to
mankind. Today one of the outstanding medical schools in this
country bears his name.

Einstein's relationship with physicians was intimate, far
reaching, and unique. He often joked about liking his doctor

friends "but not their medicine." Smiling, Einstein said, "One can die without the help of a doctor." Or "If one is ill he either gets better or he dies." Einstein was uneasy about complicated biological processes that could not be expressed mathematically. Yet his medical friends were dear to him. Physicians involved themselves with people more than men of other professions did, and the experiences between human beings interested Einstein greatly. In a way, he thought of himself as a doctor, one who tried to better human society. Because of his compassion for the individual and humanity as a whole, Einstein would have been the ideal physician.

10

Accomplishments

The accomplishments of Newton and Einstein were not limited to mathematics and physics. A glance at a list of their achievements immediately reveals why their reputations reached legendary heights. To state the case plainly, one could say that Newton was a mathematician, an experimental and theoretical physicist, an instrument maker, a chemist and a theologian. He succeeded while working in almost complete isolation for years and also as an executive directing a large governmental agency. Einstein was a theoretical physicist, a philosopher and a humanitarian. He devoted his life to the study of nature and the problems of mankind without regard for his material needs. He was the only physicist to receive the Nobel Prize for work done in his spare time at home, entirely on his own, unaffiliated with a university or research group.

Newton

Theoretical Physics

Philosophiae Naturalis Principia Mathematica, or simply the *Principia*, was published in 1687 when Newton was 44. Written in Latin and consisting of three parts, it was the first textbook on theoretical physics. In the *Principia*, Newton summarized many of his earlier findings and set forth in detail for the first time some of the laws of nature. He described mathematically the physical phenomena of mass, motion, and gravity. He gave proofs in the form of classical geometry, although undoubtedly he did not derive them initially by that method. He must have used analytical geometry and calculus, with which he was well equipped. There is good evidence that he intended to make the work difficult to avoid pursuit by "smatterers" in mathematics. He was also compulsive enough to try the more challenging geometric method to test his ingenuity. Of the mathematics that Newton used, Whewell said, "Nobody since Newton has been able to use geometric methods to the extent for the like purposes! And as we read the *Principia* we feel as when we are in an ancient armory where the weapons are of gigantic size! And as we look at them we marvel what manner of man he was who could use as a weapon what we can scarcely lift as a burden."

What Newton explained in the *Principia* is outlined below.

> Book I: *A First Book on Theoretical Mechanics*
> 1. Laws of motion.
> 2. Composition of forces.
> 3. The inverse square law describing the attraction between masses and the movement of the planets in elliptical orbits with the sun at one focus.

4. Proof that if every point attracts every other point according to the inverse square law, the attractive mass of a homogeneous sphere may be considered to be at the center.
5. Solution to the problem of motion of two bodies mutually gravitating.
6. The laws of impact of two bodies.

Book II: *A First Book of Hydrodynamics*
1. The motion of real liquids as well as the motion of bodies of various shapes through a resisting liquid, with resistance varying as the square of the velocity.
2. The solid of revolution of least resistance.
3. Mathematical description of wave motion.

Book III: *The Major Part of the Principia*
1. The movement of satellites around their planets and of the planets around the sun on the basis of universal gravitation.
2. How to find the masses of the planets in terms of the earth's mass. From an assumed estimate of the earth's density, calculations of the mass of the sun and of the planets which have satellites.
3. Quantitative account of the flattened figure of the earth.
4. Calculation of the conical motion of the earth's axis (precession of the equinoxes).
5. Analysis of the main irregularities of the moon's motion due to the pull of the sun.
6. The foundation for the theory of tides.
7. The orbits of comets and illustration of their movement under the sun's attraction so that their return could be calculated.

Experimental Physics

Newton belonged to the very small group of physicists who could switch successfully back and forth from theoretical to experimental work. He discovered that sunlight could be refracted as it passed through a prism and separated into different colors. Measuring the quality we now designate as wave length, he showed that every spectral color is characterized by a definite wave length. Newton explained rainbows, and the color of thin films, and measured interference properties of light. He defined color mixtures, and the addition and subtraction of colors. He studied the characteristics of binocular vision. He enunciated the law of cooling: the rate of cooling of a body is proportional to the difference in temperature between the body and air.

Instruments Designed

Newton made the first reflecting telescope, casting and polishing the mirror and preparing his own alloy. He invented a sextant—an important instrument for surveying and navigation—made a burning glass of seven lenses, designed a thermometer, and created and improved ear trumpets.

Mathematics

Newton's extraordinary prowess as a mathematician enabled him to solve any problem that he or others could conceive. He is best known for originating differential and integral calculus and the binomial theorem, but he also advanced other branches of mathematics. He knew how to use the calculus of variations and of finite differences. A masterful geometer, he made fundamental contributions to geometry as well as to algebra and the infinite series. He laid the basis of algebraic projective geometry.

Chemistry

Newton was an alchemist. Chemistry as we know it today did

not exist in his time. His notes on transmutation of metals and other alchemical works totaled some half-million words. Only now are students analyzing his records in detail.

Administration

Newton held several administrative posts. Twice he served as a member of parliament, and for many years he directed the Royal Mint. He worked as a consultant for a mathematics curriculum at Christ's hospital and presided over the Royal Society for 24 years.

Theology

Newton's interest in theology is discussed in a separate chapter.

Miscellaneous

Extending his interest in chronology, Newton suggested a new calendar: 6 winter months of 30 days each, 5 summer months of 31 days each, and 1 summer month of 30 days, except for 31 days in leap year.

Newton helped at least four promising young mathematicians obtain satisfactory positions. Roger Cotes (1682-1716), with Newton's support, was appointed the first Plumian Professor of Astronomy and Experimental Philosophy at the University of Cambridge. Later Cotes edited the second edition of the *Principia*. Henry Pemberton (1694-1771) was a physician who became interested in mathematics and edited the third edition of the *Principia*. Colin Maclaurin (1698-1746), a brilliant Scottish mathematician, became an assistant and later a successor to the aging James Gregory. James Stirling (1692-1770), a Scottish mathematician, fled to Venice after taking part in the Jacobite rebellion of 1715. Newton secured pardon for Stirling, gave him money, and arranged for publication of his work.

Einstein

Theoretical Physics

A. Development of the quantum theory
   1. Generalized Planck's concept of black body radiation, in which energy is composed of discrete quanta, to include light.
   2. Explained the photoelectric effect and fluorescence.
   3. Characterized stimulated emission which in turn made possible the development of lasers and masers.
   4. Formulated the "Bose-Einstein" statistics from the principles of wave mechanics to describe a group of particles indistinguishable from one another, for example, photons and alpha particles.

B. The special and general theories of relativity
   1. Showed for the first time that mass was related to energy by the formula $E = mc^2$ in which c is the velocity of light.
   2. Predicted correctly that gravity would deflect light.
   3. Refined the explanation of the movement of the planets Mercury, Venus, and Earth and obtained values that agree with experimental data.
   4. Predicted that in a gravitational field, radiant energy would show a shift in its measured frequencies. Observations made with light and gamma rays fully supported his views.
   5. Showed that the rate at which time passes varies with the velocity of motion.
   6. Predicted the presence of gravitational waves (not confirmed).

C. Developed the unified field theory to describe the characteristics of gravitational, electromagnetic and quantum phenomena. This theory has not been confirmed.

D. Atomic theory and thermodynamics
  1. Interpreted the essence of Brownian movement.
  2. Improved the analysis of the sky's blue color by including a statistical calculation of the effect of small scale fluctuations on the density of air.
  3. Developed a theory of specific heat.
  4. Described the condensation of a perfect gas at low temperature.
  5. Derived an equation for the viscosity of sols.
  6. Worked out an equation for diffusion of particles.

Einstein's entrance into quantum physics came about in the following way. To explain how a black body radiates heat, Planck in 1900 dared to assume that energy is released in discrete units or quanta and not continuously. His view, now known to be correct, had little support from other physicists after it was announced. Einstein, however, realized that if all forms of energy, including light, were composed of quanta, many experimental observations could be easily explained. By extending to light the quantum interpretation of heat, Einstein distinguished the essential character of the photoelectric effect and fluorescence. When light of suitable wave length strikes a piece of metal or a compound, electrons or light are emitted in definite quanta. Hertz was the first to note that electrons are released when light acts on some metals. His student, Lenard, extended the initial observation when he found that by increasing the intensity of the light striking the metal, more electrons could be produced but not with greater energies. Einstein solved the paradox. He explained how light of a given frequency could be absorbed only in a definite order by the metal. Likewise the incident light could induce change in energy levels within the metal resulting in emission of electrons that had specific energy. More light produced more electrons but all of the same energy. It was for this work that he received the Nobel Prize.

Light held a special fascination for Einstein. He kept returning to the study of its properties although he, like Newton, felt that gravitation was more important. In 1917 he completed a major piece of work that later became the foundation for the development of lasers and masers. When excited atoms fall to lower energy levels, radiation is emitted at random. Each kind of atom can be considered to have an average lifetime in the excited state. Einstein proposed that the descent from an excited state, in addition to occurring randomly, could be initiated by radiation of appropriate frequency to give light by stimulated emission. He showed that there is just one way to excite an atom through radiation, namely, by introducing a quantum of radiant energy. However, for de-excitation two processes exist—spontaneous or stimulated emission of a quantum. Because the former was generally much more important, the latter was temporarily forgotten. But by devising techniques to produce only stimulated emission, man has been able to make powerful lasers and masers.

A puzzle of quite a different nature inspired Einstein to create the special theory of relativity. In 1887 Michelson and Morley measured carefully the speed of light along two equal paths perpendicular to each other. The velocities were identical. If the earth moved through an ether, the speed of light should be greater when the earth moves with the ether than against it. The discrepancy between theory and experimental findings led Einstein to assume that the speed of light in a vacuum is the same for observers, whether moving or not, and that time varies with the speed of the observer. To reach such conclusions, Einstein had to reinterpret our everyday notions that time and space are separate and fuse them into a single concept. By modifying the reference of measurement, Einstein could explain the Michelson-Morley experiment and, in addition, show that mass and energy relate to one another through the simple equation $E = mc^2$ (where c is the speed of light). Deduction of this equivalence principle was an intellectual feat. However, the direction taken by experimental physics would have led to the development of atomic energy without Einstein's equation. The order would have been reversed. That is, experiments would have shown that all the energy in a nuclear reaction in which a change in mass occurred came from conversion of the mass to energy. Experiments on radioactive decay already had shown that a huge amount of energy was available in the atomic nucleus. The energy from the first atomic explosion came from the binding energy of the atomic nucleus and not directly from a transmutation of mass into energy. But since the binding energies of the particles do show up in their masses, the release of energy is indirectly connected with a change in mass of the nucleus.

Around 1908 Einstein began to seriously consider formulating the laws of gravity by extending the concepts used in the special theory of relativity. In 1916 he was able to announce the general theory of relativity. The nature and laws of gravity were stated clearly while ample room was left for the exposition of electromagnetic fields. Equations good for all systems related to one another by continuous coordinate transformations were developed. Conclusions drawn from Einstein's concept are that (1) light is deflected by a gravitational field; (2) the frequency of radiant energy shifts in a gravitational field; (3) movements of planets can be described accurately; (4) gravitational waves should exist. All but the last point agree with experimental observations. The existence of gravitation waves is currently being investigated.

By 1929 Einstein was able to make generalizations that embraced gravitation, electromagnetism, and quantum phenomena within a single theory—the unified field theory. Further improvements came in 1949, 1950, and 1953. Einstein knew that the mathematical parts of the theory were correct, but he was not sure about the physical aspects. He did not solve the equations or offer suggestions for testing the theory by experiment.

The verification of atomic theory by giving a mathematical description of Brownian movement was a scientific vignette; it showed Einstein's range, ingenuity, and skill with statistics. Most scientists already supported the atomic theory of matter, but after 1905 the last skepticism disappeared. In 1828 the English botanist, Robert Brown, first observed the random movement of small particles in water. Without knowing the details of Brownian motion, Einstein, using the general principles of thermodynamics, described mathematically the characteristics of the motion of small particles bombarded by rapidly moving water molecules. His analysis permitted a direct observation of the atomic quality of matter for the first time. Einstein's equations could be used to work out the size of molecules. Within three years, Perrin experimentally confirmed the theoretical considerations and obtained the first good values of atomic size.

Although Einstein received no challenges comparable to the puzzles Newton got from Bernoulli and Leibniz, something similar illustrates Einstein's acumen for theoretical work. Writing from memory in correspondence with Schroedinger, Einstein criticized a formula which Schroedinger did not write and then proceeded to derive the real Schroedinger equation.

Einstein, at 52, played the violin at a benefit concert in a Berlin Synagogue in 1932. A year later he emigrated to the United States. He never returned to Europe.

On Sunday, May 28, 1939, Einstein and his sister, Maja, dedicated the Jewish Pavilion at the New York World's Fair. The inscription is from Psalm 137, 5. Written after the fall of Jerusalem in 587 B.C., these words voiced the feelings of the captured Jews as they were led to Babylon.

Einstein at age 61 at the Institute of Advanced Study in Princeton. Photograph by Lucien Aigner

112 Mercer Street, Einstein's home in Princeton, New Jersey

Einstein, Princeton, New Jersey, 1945. The original mosaic, by Elsa Schmid, is in color.

William Stukeley

John Locke

Max Talmey

Moritz Katzenstein

Heinrich Zangger

Hans Mühsam

Rudolf Richard Ehrmann

Gustav Bucky

Janos Plesch

Gabriel Segall

Otto Juliusburger

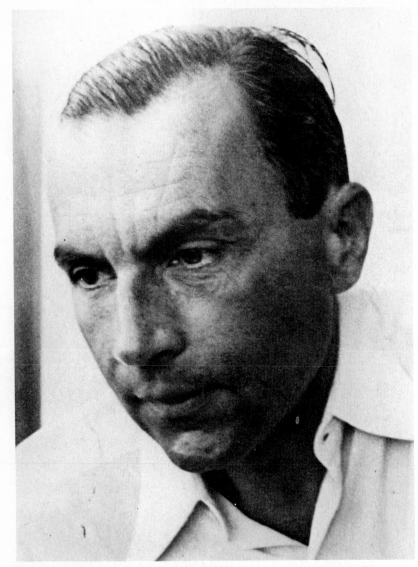

Rudolf Nissen

The photograph that Einstein sent to Dr. Nissen. The autograph reads:

> To Nissen my tummy,
> the world my tongue.

Reverend Victor S. Daws of the Rectory at Colsterworth pauses at the threshold of Woolsthorpe Manor, the house in which Sir Isaac was born. Most of the visitors to this house are Americans and French rather than English.

Elsbeth and Marcel Grossmann, daughter and son of Einstein's long-time friend Marcel Grossmann

Schroedinger glowed when he received Einstein's independent confirmation, "Your approval and Planck's mean more to me than that of half the world."

Experimental Physics

Einstein did not carry out any experiments. However, he followed technical science closely and did the following:

1. With the Habicht brothers, he invented an apparatus to measure small voltages.
2. Einstein and Leo Szilard designed a pump for liquid metals.
3. He helped Dr. Gustav Bucky construct an automatic camera.
4. For seven years, Einstein worked in a patent office examining patent applications.
5. He served as an expert patent consultant for at least two German industrial companies, preparing claims and appearing in court during their infringement cases.

Humanitarian Activities

Einstein nobly defended the downtrodden. He espoused his views without regard to any adverse effect they might have on himself.

The only time he veered from ardent pacifism occurred during the Second World War when he considered the situation with Germany desperate. His letter to President Roosevelt initiated our development of atomic energy. Einstein wrote many letters, granted interviews on peace, and loyally supported a world federation. When he was an old man, he gave a violin recital to collect money for the Children's Aid Fund. He also helped at a United States government bond rally.

Einstein's works were published not only in journals for physicists but also in books, periodicals, and newspapers for the laity. He would write a statement on Edison for *Science*, another on Nernst for *Scientific Monthly*, a criticism of the political attitudes in Russia for The *New York Times*, a plea for peace and a Christmas message for the general news services, an article on space-time for Encyclopedia Britannica, etc.

Support for the Jews and views on religion

Einstein spoke out in support of the Jewish people more than any other Jewish leader in science did in his day. After the First World War, Einstein championed a Jewish homeland in Palestine—at a time when it was fashionable for the intellectual Jews of Germany to be antizionist and nationalistic about Germany. Years later he was offered the presidency of Israel but could not accept it. His first trip to the United States was with Chaim Weizmann to collect money for the Jewish National Fund and for the Hebrew University. In 1933, when Einstein became a permanent resident of the United States, he played the violin at a rally to raise funds for victims of Nazism.

Although Jewish causes were close to his heart, he disliked strong nationalistic views. He could not understand why one would want to join a political party instead of thinking for himself.

On religion, Einstein stood in intimate relation to the God of Spinoza. Everyone who knew Einstein considered him a man of piety although he did not believe in a personal God. His lifelong zeal in trying to express the physical laws of nature within the framework of a single concept, the unified field theory, was analogous to the discovery by the ancient Hebrews of the He-Who-Is-One concept of the deity.

Support of other scientists

Einstein always sympathized with the Jewish students who had trouble obtaining an education in Eastern Europe. He helped all he could directly and indirectly, and some of the young scientists became his assistants.

In his early years of university life as a professor of theoretical physics, he often lectured and met with the students. One of his graduate students, Otto Stern, received the Nobel Prize in physics. When Einstein went to Berlin in 1914, however, his teaching responsibilities decreased.

Einstein played a key role in attracting world recognition to new concepts that he did not originate. For example, by making early use of Louis de Broglie's PhD thesis on wave mechanics, Einstein paved the way for rapid developments in this major field.

Comparison

In academic circles one may hear that a faculty member did not receive a deserved promotion because he lacked sufficient publications. The man's work is said to be excellent, but because of the thoroughness of his investigation, as well as the time devoted to teaching and administrative duties, he published few papers. Although each case must be considered separately, a university could use Einstein and Newton as examples of how quality and quantity go together. Their prodigious writing—original papers, books, letters, notes on their own work, unpublished manuscripts—was far greater than that of most other scientists. True, they did little teaching, but their writings on nonscientific subjects more than made up for time others spend in teaching and administration.

Would the accomplishments of Einstein and Newton have been made if neither had lived? With one possible exception, the answer is yes. A scientist is not a musician, artist, or poet. Nobody but Mozart could have written music exactly like his. But in science, one is seeking only the workings of nature, and step by step they are discovered. Great scientists take a lot of steps and take them earlier than others. But even without the great ones, the way eventually would be found. Einstein recognized this point, accepted it, but with one reservation—the general theory of relativity. He considered that work, which others believe is man's finest creation of abstract thought, to be like a musical composition, a painting, or a poem. The answers would have come forth without him but in a different way. The form they took belonged to him.

11

Summing Up

From all that is known of the lives of these great scientists, what did they share? It is not difficult to list the fortuitous events. Each was a first-born child and a male, followed by a sister. Each mother was pregnant with her son at approximately the same time of year. Had Newton not been premature, the month and day of his birth would have been close to Einstein's. The mothers went through a crucial first third of pregnancy in the months of June, July, and August—a period when they were least likely to catch viral infections. The boys grew up in small, quiet families uncluttered by large numbers of children. They did not play with youngsters their own age. Economically, their families were neither rich nor poor but middle class. No relatives achieved distinction. Superior educational direction came from people other than the parents, that is, individuals not involved with routine disciplining of the children: for Newton, the Clark brothers and Henry Stokes; for Einstein, Uncle Jakob and Max Talmey. Neither child's genius was recognized until the age of 12 or 13 years.

The boys attended good colleges but not the best available in their day. Excellent students, but not at the top of their classes, they did not set scholastic records. But they acted like graduate and not undergraduate students from the day they entered college. Both devoted a tremendous amount of time to subjects unrelated to the required class assignments. It seems that regular course work was a nuisance to be tolerated. In college years, as in childhood, they had the good fortune to receive invaluable assistance from a teacher or friend. The able mathematician, Isaac Barrow, recognized and nurtured Newton's genius. Einstein had his brilliant fellow student, Marcel Grossmann. The dedication toward self-motivated interests, which they expressed in college, continued after they received their bachelor's degrees and were forced out of university life. In the long, quiet, free spell away from academia, they laid the basis for their greatest contributions. They possessed the talent, drive, and persistence to follow up their early findings with years of hard work when the opportunity arose to return to a university or research institute. Again the right people came along—for Newton, Edmund Halley; for Einstein, Heinrich Zangger, Max Planck, Walter Nernst, and Hendrik Lorentz.

Much credit must be given to their own people—the English helped Newton and the Jews backed Einstein. After being at the university for several years, Newton left Cambridge without regret to work at the mint. He had been treated exceptionally well. Cambridge did everything right. At the age of 26, he was given a major professorship and was left entirely free to do what he wanted. Einstein received support from his fellow Jews all his life. His boyhood mentor, Max Talmey, was Jewish. The family structure enabled him to go to college because of financial help from two uncles whom he did not even know well. Support for Newton and Einstein, and recognition from their own people, became unlimited after they made their mark in science.

During most of their lives, Einstein and Newton enjoyed excellent health and were not handicapped by medical problems. They did not drink alcoholic beverages except on rare occasions. Their personal needs were small and their family obligations limited. Neither physicist went out of his way to seek members of the opposite sex. Newton remained a bachelor and celibate. Einstein married twice and fathered two children. His first wife was a college classmate and the second a five-years-older cousin who invited him to share her apartment. He moved in only because he was ill and needed care. They married two years later.

Although strikingly different in some ways—Newton was vain and suspicious, and Einstein had great wit—they shared major characteristics. Hardworking lone wolves, fired with curiosity and an unusual ability to concentrate and teach themselves, they were innately endowed to handle any kind of intellectual work. Completely independent in thought and action, they evaluated every situation to their own satisfaction. A deep sense of religion was tied into their work. Both had high moral standards. Their output in diverse fields was enormous, and neither had trouble writing up his results. Newton probably wrote more, but Einstein published more. The discrepancy does not reflect better printing facilities in Einstein's time but rather the completely different attitudes the two men had. Newton rarely published without persuasion. He wanted no arguments about his work. Einstein, once he completed something, wanted it made generally available. He did not worry about adverse remarks. He was harsh in his self-criticism before submitting his findings for publication. He had his views; others were entitled to theirs. Few scientists have equaled the writing productivity of these men.

One attribute of both men is of special interest. Equipped with talent and the ability to work hard, they did not engage in competition such as sports or chess. Achievement resulting from getting the better of someone else had no value. They were having a difficult enough time formulating the laws of nature.

Neither man found his work easy or thought he was unusually bright. Newton considered mathematics dry. Einstein said, "If only the development of the thought did not come up against such infamous mathematical difficulties." Newton complained that the hours concentrated on lunar theory gave him a headache and insomnia. Einstein made it clear that his results did not come easily when he commented on intellectual work, "Whoever knows it, does not go tearing after it." He wrote to a friend, "I have once more broken a little ground in the gravitational theory and by so doing have run the risk of being placed in a mad house." Newton did not attribute his success to great ability but to his capacity for staying with a problem, 24 hours a day if necessary, until it was solved. Einstein said, "I have no particular talent. I am merely extremely inquisitive." Another time, "I am perfectly aware that I do not have any special talent. Interest, devotion, and stubborn endurance coupled with self-criticism have led me to my ideals."

Their genius did not show up or went unrecognized at the ages of five or six. It is often said that they developed late, after college. Both Einstein and Newton, however, showed unusual ability by adolescence—long before college. Only a rare teen-ager thinking hard about a problem would begin a seven-mile journey home by walking his horse up a hill, forget to mount the animal after reaching a plateau, and complete the distance on foot. Some evenings Newton ended up with the bridle in his hand while the horse found his way home. When a storm is brewing, how many youths would forsake the livestock and the barns and calculate the speed of the wind instead of becoming excited over the damage about to occur? Few children begin secondary school at the bottom of the class and, because of a relatively simple challenge, rise rapidly to the top and stay there. Similar stories about Einstein abound. Several weeks after receiving a compass at the age of five, he wondered how it worked. He undoubtedly never ceased trying to solve that problem. An ordinary eleven-year-old child cannot prove that for any right triangle the square of the hypotenuse is equal to the sum of the squares of the other two sides. Most boys be-tween 12 and 16 play with children their own age, do not limit their reading to serious books on mathematics, philosophy or science, learn algebra from a textbook, or solve all the problems in the book. How many teach themselves differential and inte-gral calculus in high school when other students are not even aware of the subjects? Singular maturity is required for a lad of 15, without family encouragement, to give up the citizenship of his country of birth because of its military aspects and school system. Despite statements to the contrary, indications are good that both Einstein and Newton showed uncommon char-acteristics at an early age. Each could work extremely hard in areas of his own choosing.

To say that one man had more genius than the other is not

reasonable. Some have claimed that Newton's findings for his day were more revolutionary than Einstein's. Others have said that Einstein's work is so much more abstract than Newton's that it represents a greater achievement. Such comparisons are meaningless.

Each man possessed an intuitive feeling for physics. The inverse-square law represented no special achievement for Newton. Being the mathematician that he was, the law seemed obvious. Much more difficult was his proof that, if the law held, the planets would travel around the sun in an ellipse. He sensed the solution before he could work out the steps to get there. The same held true for Einstein. He knew in his teens that something was wrong in the interpretation of the velocity of light with regard to the speed of an observer. Also he did not see how the inverse-square law could have been derived on a logical basis. Both men had the requirements of talent, drive, and endurance to solve the problems that they initiated.

For each man, physics was the major attraction, particularly gravity and light. But their approaches differed. Newton, the supreme mathematician, used his talent to formulate the laws of nature, which interested him more than mathematics. Einstein, the elite philosopher of reason, found the precise formulations of physical principles inseparable from the most intricate mathematics. Both men were theoreticians of the lab and not the ivory tower. That is, their objectives related to practical problems, not in an engineering sense, but in order to understand nature. They were not interested in intellectual achievement for its own sake. When Newton needed the mathematics necessary to deal with acceleration, he invented differential calculus. Einstein used intricate and obscure forms of mathematics for his gravitational theory because nothing else would do.

During the last three hundred years, several men have excelled in abstract thought: Maxwell, Lorentz, Gibbs, Gauss, Bohr, Planck, von Neumann, Landau, Dirac and others. But Einstein and Newton were greater still in their overall range. Hence, even under ideal conditions, the chance of another person's fitting into the Einstein-Newton category is remote but not impossible. The unusual combination of the right aptitude, home life, interest, drive, health, opportunities, and luck in meeting helpful people at the crucial time is not an everyday occurrence. The likelihood of discovering talent should be easier today because more people are in science. Yet it is also more difficult to be isolated and entirely free to pursue one's own dreams and to exercise independent control over one's own genius for several consecutive years as were Einstein and Newton.

Residences of Newton in England
and of Einstein in central Europe

LIFE OUTLINES

year	Albert Einstein	age	Isaac Newton	year
1879	Born in Ulm, Germany, March 14, when his mother was 20 and his father 32. Father ran a small electrical engineering shop.		Born in Woolsthorpe, England, December 25, when his father, a farmer, was 36; mother's age not known. Father died several months before Isaac's birth. Isaac was a premature baby and very small.	1642 1643
1880	Family moved to Munich.	1		1644
1881	Sister Maja was born.	2		1645
1882	Slow in learning to talk.	3	Mother remarried to Rev. Barnabas Smith on January 27. Isaac lived with grandmother and uncle.	1646
1883		4	Half-sister, Mary Smith, born. Isaac went to day school in Skillington and Stoke.	1647
1884	Played with a compass while ill and was enchanted with it for a long time. Until age 9 he attended a Catholic elementary school in Munich.	5		1648
1885	Began taking violin lessons and later mastered the instrument. Music became an inner necessity.	6		1649

1886		7		1650	Half-brother, Benjamin Smith, born.
1887	Violin lessons were discontinued, but he taught himself both violin and piano.	8		1651	
1888	He still lacked fluency of speech.	9		1652	Half-sister, Hannah Smith, born.
1889	Entered Luitpold Gymnasium in Munich. Max Talmey, a 21-year-old medical student, introduced Albert to a wide range of popular and technical books on science, mathematics, and philosophy. Talmey was the first person to recognize "the boy's exceptional intelligence."	10		1653	
1890	Solved the Pythagorean theorem on his own.	11	Enrolled at King's School in Grantham. Isaac lived with Ralf Clark, the apothecary. Clark's brother, a physician, taught the boy mathematics. Mr. John Stokes was the school's headmaster. All three men recognized Isaac's oustanding abilities.	1654	
1891	Read a book on Euclidian plane geometry. Taught himself mathematics, including calculus.	12		1655	
1892	Read many books on science. Became a good violinist.	13	Stepfather, Barnabas Smith, died.	1656	

year	Isaac Newton	age	Albert Einstein	year
1657		14		1893
1658	Isaac left King's School to help family on the farm.	15	Left school to join his parents in Milan, Italy. Did not like school and the teachers did not like him. He planned to give up his German citizenship.	1894
1659		16	Albert wanted to enter the Federal Institute of Technology in Zurich. Since he had no high school diploma, he was required to take a college entrance exam. His test scores in modern languages, zoology, and botany were unsatisfactory but were outstanding in mathematics and physics. He was advised to complete secondary schooling and to return the following year.	1895
			Became a pupil in the 3rd and 4th class in the technical department of the Aarau Cantonal School. He liked this school but tended to be a loner. He read Kant's *Critique of Pure Reason*. Made kites for children. Met Paul Winteler who later married his sister. A fellow classmate considered	

Year	Age	Einstein	Newton	Year
		him a keen critic. Chose theoretical physics to be his field of work. First became interested in problems of relativity. The family persuaded the mother's brothers to pay for Albert's college education.		
1896	17	Entered the Federal Institute of Technology to study mathematical physics. Fellow classmate, Marcel Grossmann, recognized Einstein's talents. Hermann Minkowski and Adolf Hurwitz were his teachers in mathematics.	Isaac's mother gave in to pressure from John Stokes and sent him back to King's School.	1660
1897	18	Met Michele Angelo Besso. Read book by Ernst Mach that shook his faith in classical mechanics. At college he worked much of the time in the physics laboratory. At home he studied the works of Maxwell, Boltzmann, Helmholtz, Hertz, Kirchhoff, and others.	Graduated from King's School as top student. Engaged to Miss Storey. Entered Trinity College, Cambridge, June 5.	1661
1898	19		Read Kepler on optics.	1662
1899	20	Passed the intermediate examinations at college with the aid of Marcel Grossmann's notes. Spent a summer	Isaac Barrow became his teacher of natural philosophy and optics. Mastered Decartes' Analytical Geometry.	1663

year	Albert Einstein	age	Isaac Newton	year
	holiday with his sister and mother in Switzerland.			
1900	Graduated from the Federal Institute of Technology. Read the works of Minkowski. At a part time job, he did calculations on sun spots for the director of the Federal Observatory. Unable to get a university assistantship. Max Planck published his findings on energy quanta. Einstein began to be involved with theoretical problems of his own selection.	21	Elected Scholar of Trinity College. Developed the binomial theorem. Bought a prism and made observations on the refraction of light. Made first version of reflecting telescope. Went through a period of nervous fatigue from excessive work and late hours while observing a comet. From this experience, he learned to get some sleep every night.	1664
1901	Published his first paper which was concerned with capillary phenomena. Began making plans to study for a PhD degree and to work in the field of molecular attraction. He already had "a few wonderful ideas" on the inner relationship of molecular forces to the Newtonian remote forces. Became a citizen of Zurich.	22	Took his BA degree at Cambridge. Wrote his first thoughts on calculus. Went home to Woolsthorpe because of the Plague.	1665

| 1665 | 22 | During 1665 and 1666 he wrote five papers on mathematics. |
| 1901 | 22 | Obtained a five-month position to teach mathematics at the Winterthur Technical School. He also taught at a school in Schaffhausen. |

Mileva Maric was graduated from the Institute of Technology.

Einstein wrote out the formula: A (success) $= X$ (work) $+ Y$ (play) $+ Z$ (keep your mouth shut).

| 1666 | 23 | Began to think of gravity reaching to the moon. Deduced the inverse square law of gravity from Kepler's work. Worked on the composition of light. |
| 1902 | 23 | Published two papers on thermodynamics. Began work as a technical expert in the Swiss patent office in Berne. This job was obtained with the help of Marcel Grossmann's father and lasted until 1909 when Einstein was 30 years old. Working conditions were pleasant. He always referred to this position as his "cobbler's job." In his spare time he worked on his own problems in theoretical physics. |

Einstein also gave private lessons in mathematics and physics, but he had only one student—Maurice Solovine. Einstein, Solovine and Conrad Habicht constituted a private "Academy" of which Einstein was the "president." They covered the works of David

year	Isaac Newton	age	Albert Einstein	year
			Hume, Ernst Mach, John Stuart Mill, Plato, Henri Poincaré, Richard Dedekind, and others. Hume's work had the greatest effect. Einstein was influenced by Spinoza's writings. In April Dr. Max Talmey visited Einstein's parents in Milan. He found the father seriously ill and the parents reticent to talk about Albert. Dr. Talmey went on to Berne to see Albert. He received a reprint of Einstein's first paper. Met Dr. Heinrich Zangger. Although Einstein could not obtain the lowest academic post, his reputation for being unusually able was already known. When Dr. Zangger of Zurich wanted the solution to a problem in applied mathematics, he was told to see Einstein.	
1666		23	Einstein's father died in Milan at age 55. Hermann Minkowski left the Institute of Technology to take a position in Göttingen.	1902

1667	24	Returned to Cambridge as a Minor Fellow. He had by this time laid the foundations of his work on the calculus, the nature of white light, and universal gravitation and its consequences. Engagement to Miss Storey ended about this time.	1903	Published another paper on thermodynamics. Married classmate, Mileva Maric, age 27. Conrad Habicht and Maurice Solovine were witnesses at the wedding. The "Academy" was enlarged to include a second private student, Lucien Chavan, and Conrad Habicht's brother, Paul.
1668	25	Appointed Major Fellow at Cambridge. Received Master of Arts degree. Made first reflecting telescope; he cast the mirror and polished it. Made his own alloy for the instrument. He taught himself to grind non-spherical lenses.	1904	Published a paper on the molecular theory of heat. On April 14, he wrote Conrad Habicht that he had "discovered in the simplest possible way the relationship between the size of the elementary quanta of matter and the wave lengths of radiation." Helped Besso get a job at the patent office. First child, Hans Albert, was born.
1669	26	Appointed Lucasian Professor of Mathematics. Gave Isaac Barrow a manuscript on calculus and the generalized binomial theorem. Edited Barrow's book on light.	1905	Published 5 papers—any of these would have made him famous. They covered the following subjects. 1. Derivation of the formula $E = mc^2$. For the first time energy and matter

year	Isaac Newton	age	Albert Einstein	year
	Began to lecture on optics (Lectures were published in 1729).		were shown to be related to one another. The basis was laid for man's use of atomic energy. 2. He explained, on the basis of Planck's quantum theory, how metals exposed to light of suitable wave lengths emit electrons. For this description of the photoelectric effect, he received the Nobel Prize in 1921. 3. Set forth the special theory of relativity (the original manuscript was destroyed by Einstein). The equations of physics were set up with the speed of light being constant. He transformed our concepts of time and space and made them dependent on one another. Einstein first communicated his views on this theory to Michele Besso. It took five or six weeks from the conception of the idea to the completion of the paper. 4. Developed an experimentally demonstrable formula for Brownian	

165

movement which afforded the best evidence for atomic theory.

5. PhD thesis at Zurich University was dedicated "To my friend, Dr. Marcel Grossmann," and concerned "A new definition of molecular dimension." Einstein's advisor, Professor Alfred Kleiner, said "The reflections and calculations contained in this work are among the most difficult in hydrodynamics."

Maurice Solovine left for Paris.

Year		Age		Year
1670	Continued experiments on properties of light. Revised Kinckhuysen's *Algebra*.	27	Promoted to expert, second class, in the patent office. Published five more papers.	1906
1671	Made second reflecting telescope to present to the Royal Society. It was received with great enthusiasm.	28	Became concerned with the unexplained motions of the planet Mercury. Published seven papers.	1907
1671		28	His application for admission to the department of theoretical physics at the University of Berne was turned down. One reviewer of his thesis	1907

year	Isaac Newton	age	Albert Einstein	year
			wrote, "I can't understand a word of what you've written here." Played second violin with a music group once a week. Met Jacob J. Laub and published three papers with him in 1908 and 1909. Hermann Minkowski lectured on "Space and Time" as part of the relativity theory and devised a simplified mathematical treatment for this subject.	
1672	Elected Fellow of the Royal Society. Sent paper to the Royal Society on the composition of sunlight. Began to correspond with Leibniz on mathematics. Wrote a second paper on calculus.	29	Published four papers including one describing an apparatus to measure small voltages that had been devised by him and the Habicht brothers several years earlier. Again applied to the University of Berne for admission to the faculty of the physics department and was accepted. He gave his first lecture to an audience of four. Minkowski wrote to the president of the Federal Institute of Technology in Zurich of the great esteem in which Einstein was held by Planck, Nernst	1908

and Lorentz—the leading theoretical physicists of the time.

Year	Age		Year	Age	
1673	30	Hair began to gray. Scottish mathematician, James Gregory visited Newton in Cambridge. Sent in his resignation to the Royal Society, but it was not accepted. He did not become an active member of the Society until his *Principia* was published in 1687. Communicated with Christian Huygens about gravity.	1909	30	Resigned from the patent office after being appointed associate professor of theoretical physics at Zurich University. Given honorary degree at Geneva University. Published four papers. Corresponded with Planck and Lorentz.
1673	30		1909	30	Planck said in a lecture, "It is hardly necessary to mention that this new interpretation of the time concept of Einstein makes the highest demands on the physicist's capacity for abstraction and powers of imagination. In daring it exceeds everything which has yet been achieved in speculative natural science." Hermann Minkowski died at age 45 in Göttingen.
1674	31	Carried out experiments on static electricity. He was allowed to retain his professor-	1910	31	Conrad and Paul Habicht describe the "Einstein-Habicht Potential Multiplicator" for which a patent was

year	Isaac Newton	age	Albert Einstein	year
	ship without taking holy orders.		applied. Second son, Eduard, was born. Einstein's sister married Paul Winteler. Six papers were published, including a major work on radiation theory.	
1675	Sent papers on light to Royal Society. He discussed interference phenomenon. Proposed his corpuscular theory of light. He measured the quantity we now designate as wave length and showed that every spectral color is characterized by a definite wave length. Spent time on chemistry experiments. Royal Society offered to keep him on as a member without having to pay dues. Visited London and went to a meeting of the Royal Society.	32	The first decisive ideas on general relativity—the effect of gravity on light—were formulated. Einstein suggested that his theory be tested at the time of a total eclipse. Published eight papers; two of them were of major importance. Left Zurich University to become professor of theoretical physics at the German University in Prague. He stayed there for 18 months. Marcel Grossmann, on the faculty at the Federal Institute of Technology in Zurich, tried to get Einstein a professorship there. Marie Curie wrote a supporting letter. Sommerfeld spoke most highly of Einstein's work. Attended Solvay conference in Brussels.	1911

1676 — 33

He found that the path of a body under a central attraction, acting in accordance with the inverse square law, would be an ellipse.
Communicated with Leibniz on the binomial theorem he worked out in 1664.
Much correspondence with Robert Hooke on light and the beginning of a long contentious period.
Cambridge University Press would not publish his edition of Kinckhuysen's *Algebra*.
Newton contributed 40 pounds toward the building of a college library.
He corresponded with Henry Oldenburg, secretary of the Royal Society, about the best apples to use to make cider.

1677 — 34

His teacher, Isaac Barrow died.
Newton was offered the position of Master of Trinity College but could not accept because he was not in holy orders.

1912

Made professor of theoretical physics at the Zurich Federal Institute of Technology. One afternoon a week he held discussions on the new developments in physics.
Corresponded with Max von Laue on x-ray diffraction.
Continued playing the violin with various groups.
Eight papers were published.

1913

A paper on the general relativity theory was published in collaboration with Marcel Grossmann. Einstein wrote the half on physical principles and Grossmann the section on advanced mathematics.
Five additional papers were published including one in which Einstein ac-

year	Isaac Newton	age	Albert Einstein	year
			knowledged Planck's support of the theory of relativity. Marie Curie visited the Einsteins in Zurich.	
1678	The secretary of the Royal Society, Henry Oldenburg, to whom Newton had sent his papers, died.	35	Appointed to a chair of theoretical physics at the Kaiser Wilhelm Institute in Berlin. Made a member of the Prussian Academy of Sciences. A group of German astronomers went to Russia to observe a total eclipse of the sun in order to test the new theory on gravity. World War I erupted the day of the eclipse and the scientists were imprisoned. Einstein signed his first political document—a pacifist statement, "Manifesto to Europeans"—originated by Dr. George F. Nicolai. Only two people besides Nicolai and Einstein signed the report. Separated from his wife and 2 sons. Mrs. Einstein and the children returned to Zurich a few weeks before World War I began.	1914

Einstein	Age	Newton
Seventeen papers and talks were given.		Corresponded with Hooke on the motion of planets. He told Hooke he was tired of science. Newton proposed an experiment to test the diurnal motion of the earth. Corresponded with Robert Boyle on the ether in space. Charles Montague, who later gave Newton a position at the Mint, matriculated at Trinity College. Newton's mother died. He nursed her during the terminal illness.
1915 — Solved some major difficulties of the general relativity theory. Published 10 papers including two of major importance. Movement of the planet Mercury was the subject of one. Participated in pacifist activities. A co-worker commented, "the celebrities crowded about him, while he always had an eye for the common man." He and Dr. Heinrich Zangger visited the French writer and pacifist, Romain Rolland, in Vevey, Switzerland. Became ill. He developed abdominal pain and lost weight. He visited with his family in Switzerland.	**36**	**1679**
1916 — His long-awaited detailed papers on general relativity, two additional principal papers, and 13 others were published. Einstein remained a strong pacifist during the war.	**37**	**1680** — Continued correspondence with Hooke and with John Flamsteed. From 1680 to 1686 Newton was in poor health.
1917 — Described the basis for laser beams. Began to study the possibility of the existence of gravitational waves. "I	**38**	**1681**

172

year	Albert Einstein	age	Isaac Newton	year
	have once more broken a little ground in the gravitation theory and by so doing have run the risk of being placed in a madhouse." Toward the end of the year he became ill again and was sick for several months with abdominal pain. He moved into the apartment of his divorced cousin, Elsa Einstein, and her two daughters. Published a total of eight papers.			
1918	Einstein and Max Born still thought that a free and democratic Germany was possible. He managed to publish 12 papers.	39	Became aware of Picard's accurate measurements of the size of the earth.	1682
1919	The British scientific expedition led by Arthur Eddington observed the total eclipse of the sun on May 29 in Principe on the West African Gulf of Guinea and also in Sobral, Brazil. Eddington in Principe got one good photograph. Careful measurements confirmed Einstein's theory. Newspaper releases on the morning of	40	John Collins died. He was a self-educated mathematician who did much to publicize Newton's work in mathematics.	1683

November 7 by the Royal Society of London on Eddington's findings made Einstein world famous. The evening before, J. J. Thompson called Einstein's work "perhaps the greatest achievement in the history of human thought." Einstein had received advanced information about Eddington's measurements in a telegram from H. A. Lorentz on September 27. Later that day, Einstein wrote the news to his mother on a postcard.

Much time was devoted to problems of international reconciliation.

Einstein began to support a Jewish homeland in Palestine. "The thing that pleases me most is the realization of a Jewish state in Palestine." Einstein had little sympathy for the assimilated Jew.

Visited family in Zurich. Divorced from his first wife Mileva and married his cousin, Elsa Einstein. He acquired 2 stepdaughters. His mother came from Switzerland to live with him in Berlin.

An Einstein Tower was erected in

year	Isaac Newton	age	Albert Einstein	year
			Potsdam. Six papers were published.	1920
1684	Edmund Halley visited Newton in Cambridge to ask what paths the planets would take if gravity obeyed the inverse square law. Newton answered without hesitation, "an ellipse," and sent Halley mathematical proof after several weeks. This question led to the work on the *Principia*. Humphrey Newton (no relation) came to work as an assistant and their association lasted five years until 1689.	41	Gave lectures in Holland, Norway, and France. Received the Barnard Medal for Science from Columbia University. Einstein thanked American and British Quakers for feeding more than half a million German children. Mother died at age 62. Published eight papers.	
1685	He showed that for the inverse square law of attraction the gravitational pull of a spherical earth was the same as it would be if the whole mass were concentrated at the center. He had not been able to clarify this essential point in 1665-1666.	42	Visited Austria, Czechoslovakia, and Amsterdam. Traveled to the United States with Professor Chaim Weizmann to collect money for the Jewish National Fund and for the Hebrew University. They sailed on the Rotterdam and arrived in New York on April 2. More than $2 million were raised. On the return trip, he visited London. Received honorary degree from	1921

1686	43	1922

Spent the entire year in Cambridge working on the *Principia*. Much correspondence with Halley.

Princeton University.
Einstein met Leo Szilard in Berlin.
Published 15 papers.

With Marie Curie and others, he became a member of the Committee on Intellectual Cooperation of the League of Nations.

Einstein no longer felt safe in Berlin. His friend, Walter Rathenau, foreign minister of Germany, was assassinated. Einstein wrote to Maurice Solovine, "anti-Semitism is very widespread."

Einstein visited Holland. Gave a talk in Paris. In the fall he began a 6-month journey to the Orient visiting Ceylon, Singapore, Hong Kong, Shanghai, and Tokyo. He developed abdominal pains while on the Japanese steamer.

Awarded the 1921 Nobel Prize in physics for his work of 1905 on the photoelectric effect.

Began work on the unified field theory.

A rather unimportant street in his home town of Ulm was named Einsteinstrasse. It was changed in 1933 by

year	Albert Einstein	age	Isaac Newton	year
	the Nazis and then back again after the war. Fourteen papers were published.			
1923	Before returning to Berlin in the spring, he visited Palestine and Spain. Traveled to Sweden to receive the Nobel Prize. Visited family in Zurich. Resigned from the Committee of Intellectual Cooperation. Thirteen papers were published.	44	*Principia*, consisting of 3 books, was published in July or August. The composition took 18 months. Newton became involved in the university's opposition to Catholic control.	1687
1924	Einstein's friend, Paul Langevin, told him about Louis de Broglie's PhD thesis on wave mechanics. Knowing de Broglie's work, and that done by the Indian physicist, Bose, Einstein formulated the statistics applicable to a group of particles indistinguishable one from the other (Bose-Einstein statistics). Again joined the Committee of Intellectual Cooperation. Attended a meeting of the committee in Geneva.	45		1688

Year	Age	Newton	Einstein	Year
1689	46	Appointed Member of Parliament for Cambridge. He held this position for 13 months from January 1689 to February 1690.	Ten papers were published. Traveled to South America. Continued work on the unified field theory. Received the Copley Medal from the Royal Society. He began to depart from the work of most theoretical physicists. Attended the fifth session of the Intellectual Cooperative Committee in Geneva. Nine publications.	1925
1690	47	Corresponded with John Locke on religious matters.	Went to Paris and to Geneva. Six papers published.	1926
1691	48		Attended Solvay conference in Brussels. Had portrait painted for the Nuremberg State Gallery. Again visited Paris. Still managed to be associated with 11 papers.	1927
1692	49	Near his 50th birthday, December 25, he developed nervous fatigue. For two years he had suffered profound melancholy, long periods of sleepless-	Hendrik Lorentz died at age 75. Einstein went to his funeral in Holland. Visited Switzerland. Became ill again and exhausted. Con-	1928

year	Isaac Newton	age	Albert Einstein	year
	ness, fears of persecution, and paranoid attitudes. However, during intervals of improvement he wrote letters to John Wallis and to Leibniz on calculus and solved the probability problem sent by Pepys.		fined to bed for 3 months. Helen Dukas became his secretary. With Leo Szilard he worked out a pump for liquid metals and applied for a patent. Published 5 papers, including the first one on the unified field theory. Accepted his election to the Board of Directors of the German League for Human Rights—a pacifist movement.	
1693	Newton experimented with thermometers.	50	The unified field theory that combines in a single concept gravitational and electromagnetic equations was published together with nine other papers. A rabbi in New York cabled, "Do you believe in God?—prepaid reply fifty words." Einstein wired back, "I believe in Spinoza's God who reveals himself in the harmony of all being, not in a god who concerns himself with the fate and actions of men." Began extensive series on interviews and correspondence on behalf of pacifism and Zionism.	1929

1930

Attended his last Solvay conference in Brussels. Visited England. Received an honorary degree from his college, the Federal Institute of Technology, in Zurich.
Left Berlin for the first of three visits at the California Institute of Technology in Pasadena.
In New York he met Arturo Toscanini, Fritz Kreisler, Nicholas Murray Butler, James J. Walker, and John D. Rockefeller, Jr.
Published 13 papers.

1931

Gave talks in California. Met Helen Keller, Charlie Chaplin, Upton Sinclair, and Norman Thomas.
Again visited England. Spoke at Oxford and received an honorary degree.
Gave many speeches on pacifism.
Completed new version of unified field theory and published a total of 12 papers.
Visited Vienna and Brussels.
In December he was off again to

51

52

Went to Paris.

1694

Continued his work on lunar theory. He corresponded with Flamsteed about the motion of the moon and visited him.
David Gregory tried to call on Newton at Cambridge but could not see him. Newton was sick, weary, and depressed.

1695

Worked on lunar theory.

year	Isaac Newton	age	Albert Einstein	year
			California. On the small ship he wrote in his diary on December 2, "I decided today that I shall essentially give up my Berlin position and shall be a bird of passage for the rest of my life." He was offered a position at the Institute for Advanced Studies in Princeton.	1932
1696	Made Warden of the Mint and began work on recoinage. Worked intermittently on lunar theory and gravity.	53	Traveled to Geneva for a peace conference. Visited Oxford. Einstein corresponded with Sigmund Freud, 76, on the reasons for war and how to prevent it. Einstein's letter and Freud's analysis are classics. Freud was not optimistic. "All my life I have had to tell people truths that were difficult to swallow. Now that I am old, I certainly do not want to fool them." In California again. Accepted the position in Princeton. Gave many interviews. Extensive correspondence including letter to Maxim Gorki.	

1933

Published eight papers.

Met Clarence Darrow. Returned to Europe. Visited Belgium. Played in a quartet with Queen Elizabeth of Belgium.

Einstein decided not to return to Berlin and went to Belgium instead. His property was confiscated by the Nazis and a price put on his head. He was offered posts in many countries. He spent June in Oxford. Met Winston Churchill and David Lloyd George. Returned to Belgium. Went to England in September before going to America.

Einstein no longer was a pacifist, and pacifist groups criticized him. Einstein gave repeated warnings to the world that Germany was preparing for war. Resigned from the Prussian Academy of Science and the Bavarian Academy of Science.

His friend, Paul Ehrenfest, committed suicide in Amsterdam at age 57.

Appointed to the faculty of the Institute for Advanced Studies at Prince-

54

1697

Met regularly with Sir Christopher Wren, John Locke, and others at the King's Library.
Solved math problems proposed by Johann Bernoulli.

year	Albert Einstein	age	Isaac Newton	year
	ton. Arrived in Princeton on October 17. He never returned to Europe. Published five papers. Gave many interviews. Wrote to old friend, Maurice Solovine. Attended dinner in New York for Nobel Prize winners.			
1934	Gave a violin recital in New York for a benefit fund to help scientists fleeing from Germany. Step daughter, Ilse, died. Published three papers.	55	Newton visited the Royal Observatory. Corresponded with John Harington about harmonic musical ratios. His niece, Catherine Barton, came to London to live with him.	1698
1935	Received honorary degree from Harvard University. Vacationed at Old Lyme, Connecticut. Wrote to his sister in Italy, "The basis of all human values is morality. The only claim to greatness of our Moses is that he saw this in primitive times." Went to Bermuda with family and Helen Dukas to conform with immigration regulations. Published three papers. Many letters and interviews.	56	Made Master of the Mint. Recoinage was completed. Continued correspondence and arguments with Flamsteed. Controversy with Leibniz began. He reviewed papers on mathematics. Suggested that a reformed calendar be used.	1699

		1936
	57	Einstein's wife, Elsa, died. Marcel Grossmann died at age 58 in Switzerland. Leopold Infeld became his assistant. Wrote to Freud on his 80th birthday. Three publications as well as several talks and interviews.
		1937
	58	Published only one paper—a major piece of work on gravitational waves. Speeches and interviews.
		1938
	59	Wrote to Maurice Solovine and to Supreme Court Justice Felix Frankfurter. Published six papers. Continued to deliver talks and interviews.
		1939
	60	At the urging of Leo Szilard and others, Einstein wrote President Roosevelt about the importance of the United States' undertaking the development of atomic energy. Einstein did not want an atom bomb

1700	Officially resigned his Cambridge professorship. Read a paper on chemistry. Described a thermometer he made several years earlier. Again represented the University of Cambridge in parliament, from February 1701 to July 1702.
1702	Visited with John Locke.
1703	Made President of the Royal Society. Robert Hooke died and Newton felt freer to publish his works. Newton may have proposed marriage to Lady Norris.

year	Isaac Newton	age	Albert Einstein	year
			to be used in warfare. However, he believed that Germany was trying to make an atomic weapon and that it was essential for the free nations to have it first. From 1914 to 1933, Einstein was an ardent, outspoken pacifist. But in 1933 he had the courage to change his view. "I am a *dedicated* but not an *absolute* pacifist; this means that I am opposed to the use of force under any circumstances, except when confronted by an enemy who pursues the destruction of life as an end in itself."	
			Sister Maja came to Princeton to live with him.	
			Wrote for time capsule at New York's World's Fair.	
			Again wrote to Freud, shortly before his death at 83. Published one paper.	
1704	Published *Opticks*, containing his major experimental works. Presented a burning glass of seven lenses to the Royal Society.	61	Became an American citizen. Einstein wrote to Roosevelt again urging a more rapid attempt to develop atomic energy.	1940

1941

Visited with son, Hans Albert, and family.
Swiss theologian, Adolf Keller, visited Einstein at Princeton.
Abdominal pain returned.
Published two papers.

62

Dr. Max Talmey, Einstein's boyhood mentor, died in New York at 74.
Gave violin concert in Princeton for the Children's Aid Fund.
Leopold Infeld described Einstein well in his book, *Quest*.
Wrote to Maxim Litvinov, Soviet ambassador to the United States, regarding international cooperation.
On December 6, the eve of Pearl Harbor, the government decided to give massive support to the development of atomic energy.
Published three papers.

1942

Einstein's second private pupil, Lucien Chavan, died in Geneva.
Self-sustaining chain reaction to produce nuclear fission achieved in Chicago, December 2.
Published two papers.

63

Controversy with Leibniz on the calculus was reviewed.
John Locke died.

1705

Knighted by Queen Anne.
Began to plan a new edition of the *Principia*.
Problems and personal discussions with Flamsteed continued.
Became a candidate for the House of Commons but was defeated.

1706

year	Isaac Newton	age	Albert Einstein	year
1707	Made a member of a committee to draw up regulations to govern a new professorship at Cambridge.	64	Einstein's graduate student, Otto Stern, received the Nobel Prize in physics. Copied by hand the original 1905 paper on the special theory of relativity to raise money for the War Bond drive. Auctioned in 1944 for 6 million dollars. Now in the Library of Congress. Became a consultant for the Navy Ordnance Bureau. Published one paper.	1943
1708		65	Wrote to Max Born that they had been naive to believe that Germany could be democratic. Voted for President Roosevelt. Einstein considered Roosevelt and Gandhi the greatest contemporary statesmen. Published three papers.	1944
1709	Sent Roger Cotes notes on *Principia* for a new edition which Cotes was to edit.	66	At Szilard's suggestion, Einstein wrote to President Roosevelt regarding future arms race. Atom bomb test a success in New	1945

			Mexico, July 16. Hiroshima bombed on August 6 and Nagasaki on August 9. Officially retired from the Institute for Advanced Studies but continued work at his office. Sent a message to the Nobel anniversary dinner at the Hotel Astor. Became very involved with world peace efforts. Published four papers.
1946	67	1710	Einstein agreed to serve as chairman of the newly formed Emergency Committee of Atomic Scientists. He corresponded with Vice-President Henry A. Wallace. Paul Langevin died in Paris at age 74. Sister Maja became bedridden. Refused to be reinstated as a member of the Bavarian Academy of Science. Continued work on the unified field theory. Published two papers.
1947	68	1711	Max Planck, age 89, died in Göttingen. Wrote open letter on peace to Russian scientists. A mathematics paper he gave Barrow in 1669 was published.

year	Isaac Newton	age	Albert Einstein	year
1712	Committee from the Royal Society completed its report on the Newton-Leibniz controversy.	69	Published one paper. First wife, Mileva, age 72, died in Zurich. Wrote to old friends of the "Academy," Maurice Solovine and Conrad Habicht. Would not become an honorary member of a German association for world government. Wrote a statement for a memorial service honoring Gandhi who had been assassinated in January. Operated on in New York as part of diagnostic workup. Was found to have a large aneurysm of the abdominal aorta. Published five papers.	1948
1713	2nd edition of *Principia* appeared. Many arguments with Flamsteed. Bernoulli wrote to Leibniz on the calculus controversy. Leibniz published a paper accusing Newton of false claims about the calculus.	70	300 scientists assembled in Princeton to hold a symposium on Einstein's contributions. I. I. Rabi said, "No other man before Einstein, or since, has delved so deeply into our most instinctive concepts of space, time and causality."	1949

		At 70 Einstein impressed mathematician Alexander Ostrowsky with his wide range of knowledge in mathematics. Continued his correspondence with Solovine. Refused offer to become a foreign scientific member of the Max Planck Institute. Would not accept honorary citizenship of Ulm—the city of his birth. Published one paper.	
1714	71	1950	Gave a five-minute nation-wide radio-TV talk to support world government. Einstein wrote to Trygve Lie, Secretary-General of the United Nations, and also to Mark Van Doren. Wrote to Miss Susanne Markwalder, daughter of the owner of the house he lived in when an undergraduate in Zurich, and with whom he played violin-piano sonatas.
1715 Charles Montague died.	72	1951	Einstein's sister, Maja, 70, died in Princeton. Wrote to Queen Elizabeth of Belgium about his progress on the unified

year	Isaac Newton	age	Albert Einstein	year
1716	Solved a problem proposed by Leibniz. Like his attack on Bernoulli's problem in 1697, Newton solved Leibniz's problem after receiving it when he arrived home from work at the mint and before going to bed. Leibniz died, but arguments regarding the origin of the calculus continued.	73	field theory. "The fascinating magic of that work will continue to my last breath." Supported Yeshiva University's ambition to establish a medical school.	1952

Chaim Weizmann died at 78. Presidency of Israel was offered to Einstein, but he did not accept it. Analysis of debris from atom bomb test of October 1952 showed the presence of element 99. In 1955 this element was named einsteinium.

Another total eclipse of the sun took place; and, as in 1919, the effect of gravity on light was found to be in accordance with Einstein's predictions. Refused to become an honorary citizen of West Berlin.

Brother-in-law, Paul Winteler, died in Geneva.

Einstein went to court as a witness for his friend, Dr. Gustav Bucky, who was suing a company for patent infringement.

1717	74	Second edition of *Opticks* appeared. He added to and modified the first edition. He suggested that telescopes be used on the highest mountains. He discussed the slit versus a hole for spectral work.	1953	74	Final paper published on the unified field theory.

1717 74 Second edition of *Opticks* appeared. He added to and modified the first edition. He suggested that telescopes be used on the highest mountains. He discussed the slit versus a hole for spectral work.

1718 75

1719 76

1953 74 Final paper published on the unified field theory.

He was certain that the mathematical concepts of the theory were correct but was not positive about the physical aspects.

Would not accept honorary membership in the German section of the International Organization of Opponents of Military Service.

Agreed to have the medical school at Yeshiva University named after him.

1954 75 Supported Robert Oppenheimer and opposed his dismissal from the Atomic Energy Commission.

Became ill in the fall and was bedridden for several weeks.

1955 76 Continued correspondence with Queen Elizabeth.

Wrote to Niels Bohr asking him to support Bertrand Russell's appeal to halt the nuclear arms race.

Michele Besso died on March 15.

During the last week of his life, Einstein dealt with subjects dearest to him—world peace, the future of the year   Isaac Newton   age   Albert Einstein   year

Jewish people, and problems in physics. Einstein's final letter was to Bertrand Russell on April 11, 1955, agreeing to his appeal. That same day the Israeli Ambassador, Abba Eban, and the Israeli Consul visited Einstein to discuss a television program to celebrate the seventh year of Israel's independence. By letter, the consul asked Einstein to give a speech on science. "So I still have a chance of becoming world-famous." Einstein agreed to the appearance but suggested that he make a more general statement pleading for peace. On the evening of the 13th he became ill and was hospitalized on April 15. "Here on earth I have done my job." He asked to have the physics formulas he was currently working on brought to the hospital. He tried to concentrate on the formulas, but abdominal pains forced him to stop. Albert Einstein died on Monday, April 18 at 1:00 A.M. of a ruptured aorta.

Year	Age	Event
1720	77	John Flamsteed died.
1721	78	First visit to Oxford.
1722	79	
1723	80	
1724		Beginning of correspondence with a French publisher about his essay, "A Short Chronicle from the First Memory of Things in Europe to the Conquest of Persia by Alexander the Great." Wrote Halley about lunar theory. Began to plan for a 3rd edition of the *Principia*. Passed 2 renal stones.
1725	82	Developed gout.
1726	83	Third edition of the *Principia*, edited by Dr. Henry Pemberton, was published.
1727		Newton died on Monday, March 20, 1727 between 1:00 and 2:00 A.M. His body lay in state in Jerusalem Chamber and he was buried in Westminster Abbey. This was the first and only time that national honors were given to a man of science, learning, or art in England.

APPENDIXES

Correspondence

Einstein to Freud

July 30, 1932

Dear Mr. Freud:

The proposal of the League of Nations and its International Institute of Intellectual Co-operation at Paris that I should invite a person, to be chosen by myself, to a frank exchange of views on any problem that I might select affords me a very welcome opportunity of conferring with you upon a question which, as things now are, seems the most insistent of all the problems civilization has to face. This is the problem: Is there any way of delivering mankind from the menace of war? It is common knowledge that, with the advance of modern science, this issue has come to mean a matter of life and death for civilization as we know it; nevertheless, for all the zeal displayed, every attempt at its solution has ended in a lamentable breakdown.

I believe, moreover, that those whose duty it is to tackle the problem professionally and practically are growing only too aware of their impotence to deal with it, and have now a very lively desire to learn the views of men who, absorbed in the pursuit of science, can see world problems in the perspective distance lends. As for me, the normal objective of my thought affords no insight into the dark places of human will and feeling. Thus, in the inquiry now proposed, I can do little more than to seek to clarify the question at issue and, clearing the ground of the more obvious solutions, enable you to bring the light of your far-reaching knowledge of man's instinctive life to bear upon the problem. There are certain psychological obstacles whose existence a layman in the mental sciences may dimly surmise, but whose interrelations and vagaries he is incompetent to fathom; you, I am convinced, will be able to suggest educative methods, lying more or less outside the scope of politics, which will eliminate these obstacles.

As one immune from nationalist bias, I personally see a simple way of dealing with the superficial (i.e., administrative) aspect of the problem: the setting up, by international consent, of a legislative and judicial body to settle every conflict arising between nations. Each nation would undertake to abide by the orders issued by this legislative body, to invoke its decision in every dispute, to accept its judgments unreservedly and to carry out every measure the tribunal deems necessary for the execution of its decrees. But here, at the outset, I come up against a difficulty; a tribunal is a human institution which, in proportion as the power at its disposal is inadequate to enforce its verdicts, is all the more prone to suffer these to be deflected by extrajudicial pressure. This is a fact with which we have to reckon; law and might inevitably go hand in hand, and juridical decisions approach more nearly the ideal justice demanded by the community (in whose name and interests these verdicts are pronounced) insofar as the community has effective power to compel respect of its juridical ideal. But at present we are far from possessing any supranational organization competent to render verdicts of incontestable authority and enforce absolute submission to the execution of its verdicts. Thus I am led to my first axiom: The quest of international security involves the unconditional surrender by every nation, in a certain measure, of its liberty of action—its sovereignty that is to say—and it is clear beyond all doubt that no other road can lead to such security.

The ill success, despite their obvious sincerity, of all the efforts made during the last decade to reach this goal leaves us no room to doubt that strong psychological factors are at work which paralyze these efforts. Some of these factors are not far to seek. The craving for power which characterizes the governing class in every nation is hostile to any limitation of the national sovereignty. This political power hunger is often supported by the activities of another group, whose aspirations are on purely mercenary, economic lines. I have especially in mind that small but determined group, active in every nation, composed of individuals who, indifferent to social considerations and restraints, regard warfare, the manufacture and sale of arms, simply as an occasion to advance their personal interests and enlarge their personal authority.

But recognition of this obvious fact is merely the first step toward an appreciation of the actual state of affairs. Another question follows hard upon it: How is it possible for this small clique to bend the will of the majority, who stand to lose and suffer by a state of war, to the service of their ambitions? (In speaking of the majority I do not exclude soldiers of every rank who have chosen war as their profession, in the belief that they are serving to defend the highest interests of their race, and that attack is often the best method of defense.) An obvious answer to this question would seem to be that the minority, the ruling class at present, has the schools and press, usually the Church as well, under its thumb. This enables it to organize and sway the emotions of the masses, and makes its tool of them.

Yet even this answer does not provide a complete solution. Another questions arises from it: How is it that these devices succeed so well in rousing men to such wild enthusiasm, even to sacrifice their lives? Only one answer is possible. Because man has within him a lust for hatred and destruction. In normal times this passion exists in a latent state, it emerges only in unusual circumstances; but it is a comparatively easy task to call it into play and raise it to the power of a collective psychosis. Here lies, perhaps the crux of all the complex factors we are considering, an enigma that only the expert in the lore of human instincts can resolve.

And so we come to our last question. Is it possible to control man's mental evolution so as to make him proof against the psychosis of hate and destructiveness? Here I am thinking by no means only of the so-called uncultured masses. Experience proves that it is rather the so-called "intelligentsia" that is most apt to yield to these disastrous collective suggestions, since the intellectual has no direct contact with life in the raw but encounters it in its easiest, synthetic form — upon the printed page.

To conclude: I have so far been speaking only of wars between nations; what are known as international conflicts. But I am well aware that the aggressive instinct operates under other forms and in other circumstances. (I am thinking of civil wars, for instance, due in earlier days to religious zeal, but nowadays to social factors; or, again, the persecution of racial minorities.) But my insistence on what is most typical, most cruel and extravagant form of conflict between man and man was deliberate, for here we have the best occasion of discovering ways and means to render all armed conflicts impossible.

I know that in your writings we may find answers, explicit or implied, to all the issues of this urgent and absorbing problem. But it would be of the greatest service to us all were you to present the problem of world peace in the light of your most recent discoveries, for such a presentation well might blaze the trail for new and fruitful modes of action.

Yours very sincerely,

A. Einstein

Freud felt that Einstein would be discouraged by his pessimistic reply, but he had to be straightforward. "All my life I have had to tell people truths that were difficult to swallow. Now that I am old, I certainly do not want to fool them."

Freud to Einstein

September 1932

Dear Mr. Einstein:

When I learned of your intention to invite me to a mutual exchange of views upon a subject which not only interested you personally but seemed deserving, too, of public interest, I cordially assented. I expected you to choose a problem lying on the borderland of the knowable, as it stands today, a theme which each of us, physicist and psychologist, might approach from his own angle, to meet at last on common ground, though setting out from different premises. Thus the question which you put me—what is to be done to rid mankind of the war menace?—took me by surprise. And, next, I was dumfounded by the thought of my (of *our*, I almost wrote) incompetence; for this struck me as being a matter of practical politics, the statesman's proper study. But then I realized that you did not raise the question in your capacity of scientist or physicist, but as a lover of his fellow men, who responded to the call of the League of Nations much as Fridtjof Nansen, the polar explorer, took on himself the task of succoring

homeless and starving victims of the World War. And, next, I remind-
ed myself that I was not being called on to formulate practical pro-
posals but, rather, to explain how this question of preventing wars
strikes a psychologist.

But here, too, you have stated the gist of the matter in your letter
—and taken the wind out of my sails! Still, I will gladly follow in
your wake and content myself with endorsing your conclusions,
which, however, I propose to amplify to the best of my knowledge
or surmise.

You begin with the relations between might and right, and this is
assuredly the proper starting point for our inquiry. But, for the term
might, I would substitute a tougher and more telling word: *violence*.
In right and violence we have today an obvious antinomy. It is easy
to prove that one has evolved from the other and, when we go back
to origins and examine primitive conditions, the solution of the problem follows easily enough. I must crave your indulgence if in what
follows I speak of well-known, admitted facts as though they were
new data; the context necessitates this method.

Conflicts of interest between man and man are resolved, in principle, by the recourse to violence. It is the same in the animal kingdom,
from which man cannot claim exclusion; nevertheless, men are also
prone to conflicts of opinion, touching, on occasion, the loftiest
peaks of abstract thought, which seem to call for settlement by quite
another method. This refinement is, however, a late development. To
start with, group force was the factor which, in small communities,
decided points of ownership and the question which man's will was
to prevail. Very soon physical force was implemented, then replaced,
by the use of various adjuncts; he proved the victor whose weapon
was the better, or handled the more skillfully. Now, for the first time,
with the coming of weapons, superior brains began to oust brute
force, but the object of the conflict remained the same: one party
was to be constrained, by the injury done him or impairment of his
strength, to retract a claim or a refusal. This end is most effectively
gained when the opponent is definitely put out of action—in other
words, is killed. This procedure has two advantages: the enemy cannot renew hostilities, and, secondly, his fate deters others from following his example. Moreover, the slaughter of a foe gratifies an
instinctive craving—a point to which we shall revert hereafter. However, another consideration may be set off against this will to kill: the
possibility of using an enemy for servile tasks if his spirit be broken
and his life spared. Here violence finds an outlet not in slaughter but

in subjugation. Hence springs the practice of giving quarter; but the victor, having from now on to reckon with the craving for revenge that rankles in his victim, forfeits to some extent his personal security.

Thus, under primitive conditions, it is superior force—brute violence, or violence backed by arms—that lords it everywhere. We know that in the course of evolution this state of things was modified, a path was traced that led away from violence to law. But what was this path? Surely it issued from a single verity: that the superiority of one strong man can be overborne by an alliance of many weaklings, that *l'union fait la force*. Brute force is overcome by union; the allied might of scattered units makes good its right against the isolated giant. Thus we may define "right" (i.e., law) as the might of a community. Yet it, too, is nothing else than violence, quick to attack whatever individual stands in its path, and it employs the selfsame methods, follows like ends, with but one difference: it is the communal, not individual, violence that has its way. But, for the transition from crude violence to the reign of law, a certain psychological condition must first obtain. The union of the majority must be stable and enduring. If its sole *raison d'être* be the discomfiture of some overweening individual and, after his downfall, it be dissolved, it leads to nothing. Some other man, trusting to his superior power, will seek to reinstate the rule of violence, and the cycle will repeat itself unendingly. Thus the union of the people must be permanent and well organized; it must enact rules to meet the risk of possible revolts; must set up machinery insuring that its rules—the laws—are observed and that such acts of violence as the laws demand are duly carried out. This recognition of a community of interests engenders among the members of the group a sentiment of unity and fraternal solidarity which constitutes its real strength.

So far I have set out what seems to me the kernel of the matter: the suppression of brute force by the transfer of power to a larger combination, founded on the community of sentiments linking up its members. All the rest is mere tautology and glosses. Now the position is simple enough so long as the community consists of a number of equipollent individuals. The laws of such a group can determine to what extent the individual must forfeit his personal freedom, the right of using personal force as an instrument of violence, to insure the safety of the group. But such a combination is only theoretically possible; in practice the situation is always complicated by the fact that, from the outset, the group includes elements of unequal power, men and women, elders and children, and very soon, as a result of war and conquest, victors and the vanquished—i.e., masters and slaves—as well. From this time on the common law takes notice of these inequalities of power, laws are made by and for the rulers, giving the servile classes fewer rights. Thenceforward there exist within the state two factors making for legal instability, but legislative evolution, too: first, the attempts by members of the ruling class to set themselves above the law's restrictions and, secondly, the constant struggle of the ruled to extend their rights and see each gain embodied in the code, replacing legal disabilities by equal laws for all. The second of these tendencies will be particularly marked when there takes place a positive mutation of the balance of power within the community, the frequent outcome of certain historical conditions. In such cases the laws may gradually be adjusted to the changed conditions or (as more usually ensues) the ruling class is loath to rush in with the new developments, the result being insurrections and civil wars, a period when law is in abeyance and force once more the arbiter, followed by a new regime of law. There is another factor of constitutional change, which operates in a wholly pacific manner, viz: the cultural evolution of the mass of the community; this factor, however, is of a different order and can only be dealt with later.

Thus we see that, even within the group itself, the exercise of violence cannot be avoided when conflicting interests are at stake. But the common needs and habits of men who live in fellowship under the same sky favor a speedy issue of such conflicts and, this being so, the possibilities of peaceful solutions make steady progress. Yet the most casual glance at world history will show an unending series of conflicts between one community and another or a group of others, between large and smaller units, between cities, countries, races, tribes and kingdoms, almost all of which were settled by the ordeal of war. Such war ends either in pillage or in conquest and its fruits, the downfall of the loser. No single all-embracing judgment can be passed on these wars of aggrandizement. Some, like the war between the Mongols and the Turks, have led to unmitigated misery; others, however, have furthered the transition from violence to law, since they brought larger units into being, within whose limits a recourse to violence was banned and a new regime determined all disputes. Thus the Roman conquest brought that boon, the *pax Romana*, to the Mediterranean lands. The French kings' lust for aggrandizement created a new France, flourishing in peace and unity. Paradoxical as it sounds, we must admit that warfare well might serve to pave the way to that unbroken peace we so desire, for it is war that brings vast empires into being, within whose frontiers all warfare is proscribed by a strong central power. In practice, however, this end is not attained, for as a rule the fruits of victory are but short-lived, the new-created unit falls asunder once again, generally because there can be no true cohesion between the parts that violence has welded. Hitherto, moreover, such conquests have only led to aggregations which, for all their magnitude, had limits, and disputes between these units could be resolved only by recourse to arms. For humanity at large the sole result of all these military enterprises was that, instead of frequent, not to say incessant, little wars, they had now to face great wars which, for all they came less often, were so much the more destructive.

Regarding the world of today the same conclusion holds good, and you, too, have reached it, though by a shorter path. There is but one sure way of ending war and that is the establishment, by common consent, of a central control which shall have the last word in every conflict of interests. For this, two things are needed: first, the creation of such a supreme court of judicature; secondly, its investment with adequate executive force. Unless this second requirement be fulfilled, the first is unavailing. Obviously the League of Nations, acting as a Supreme Court, fulfills the first condition; it does not fulfill the second. It has no force at its disposal and can only get it if the members of the new body, its constituent nations, furnish it. And, as things are, this is a forlorn hope. Still we should be taking a very shortsighted view of the League of Nations were we to ignore the fact that here is an experiment the like of which has rarely—never before, perhaps, on such a scale—been attempted in the course of history. It is an attempt to acquire the authority (in other words, coercive influence), which hitherto reposed exclusively in the possession of power, by calling into play certain idealistic attitudes of mind. We have seen that there are two factors of cohesion in a community; violent compulsion and ties of sentiment ("identifications," in technical parlance) between the members of the group. If one of these factors becomes inoperative, the other may still suffice to hold the group together. Obviously such notions as these can only be significant when they are the expression of a deeply rooted sense of unity, shared by all. It is necessary, therefore, to guage the efficacy of such sentiments. History tells us that, on occasion, they have been effective. For example, the Panhellenic conception, the Greeks' awareness of superiority over their barbarian neighbors, which found expression in the Amphictyonies, the Oracles and Games, was strong enough to humanize the methods of warfare as between Greeks, though inevitably it failed to prevent conflicts between different elements of the Hellenic race or even to deter a city or group of cities from joining forces with their racial foe, the Persians, for the discomfiture of a rival. The solidarity of Christendom in the Renaissance age was no more effective, despite its vast authority, in hindering Christian nations, large and small alike, from calling in the Sultan to their aid. And, in our times, we look in vain for some such unifying notion whose authority would be unquestioned. It is all too clear that the nationalistic ideas, paramount today in every country, operate in quite a contrary direction. Some there are who hold that the Bolshevist conceptions may make an end of war, but, as things are, that goal lies very far away and, perhaps, could only be attained after a spell of brutal internecine warfare. Thus it would seem that any effort to replace brute force by the might of an ideal is, under present conditions, doomed to fail. Our logic is at fault if we ignore the fact that right is founded on brute force and even today needs violence to maintain it.

I now can comment on another of your statements. You are amazed that it is so easy to infect men with the war fever, and you surmise that man has in him an active instinct for hatred and destruction, amenable to such stimulations. I entirely agree with you. I believe in the existence of this instinct and have been recently at pains to study its manifestations. In this connection may I set out a fragment of that knowledge of the instincts, which we psychoanalysts, after so many tentative essays and gropings in the dark, have compassed? We assume that human instincts are of two kinds: those that conserve and unify, which we call "erotic" (in the meaning Plato gives to Eros in his Symposium), or else "sexual" (explicitly extending the popular connotation of "sex"); and, secondly, the instincts to destroy and kill, which we assimilate as the aggressive or destructive instincts. These are, as you perceive, the well-known opposites, Love and Hate, transformed into theoretical entities; they are, perhaps, another aspect of those external polarities, attraction and repulsion, which fall within your province. But we must be chary of passing overhastily to the notions of good and evil. Each of these instincts is every whit as indispensable as its opposite, and all the phenomena of life derive from their activity, whether they work in concert or in opposition. It seems that an instinct of either category can operate but rarely in isolation; it is always blended ("alloyed," as we say) with a certain dosage of its opposite, which modifies its aim or even, in certain circumstances, is a prime condition of its attainment. Thus the instinct of self-preservation is certainly of an erotic nature, but to gain its end this very instinct necessitates aggressive action. In the same way the love instinct, when directed to a specific object, calls for an admixture of the acquisitive instinct if it is to enter into effective possession of that object. It is the difficulty of isolating the two kinds of instinct in their manifestations that has so long prevented us from recognizing them.

If you will travel with me a little further on this road, you will find that human affairs are complicated in yet another way. Only exceptionally does an action follow on the stimulus of a single instinct, which is *per se* a blend of Eros and destructiveness. As a rule several motives of similar composition concur to bring about the act. This fact was duly noted by a colleague of yours, Professor G. C. Lichtenberg, sometime Professor of Physics at Göttingen; he was perhaps even more eminent as a psychologist than as a physical scientist. He evolved the notion of a "Compass-card of Motives" and wrote: "The efficient motives impelling man to act can be classified like the thirty-two winds and described in the same manner; e.g., *Food-Food-Fame* or *Fame-Fame-Food*." Thus, when a nation is summoned to engage in war, a whole gamut of human motives may respond to this appeal — high and low motives, some openly avowed, others slurred over. The lust for aggression and destruction is certainly included; the innumerable cruelties of history and man's daily life confirm its prevalence and strength. The stimulation of these destructive impulses by appeals to idealism and the erotic instinct naturally facilitate their release. Musing on the atrocities recorded on history's page, we feel that the ideal motive has often served as a camouflage for the lust of destruction; sometimes, as with the cruelties of the Inquisition, it seems that, while the ideal motives occupied the foreground of consciousness, they drew their strength from the destructive instincts submerged in the unconscious. Both interpretations are feasible.

You are interested, I know, in the prevention of war, not in our theories, and I keep this fact in mind. Yet I would like to dwell a little longer on this destructive instinct which is seldom given the attention that its importance warrants. With the least of speculative efforts we are led to conclude that this instinct functions in every living being, striving to work its ruin and reduce life to its primal state of inert matter. Indeed, it might well be called the "death instinct"; whereas the erotic instincts vouch for the struggle to live on. The death instinct becomes an impulse to destruction when, with the aid of certain organs, it directs its action outward, against external objects. The living being, that is to say, defends its own existence by destroying foreign bodies. But, in one of its activities, the death instinct is operative *within* the living being and we have sought to trace back a number of normal and pathological phenomena to this *introversion* of the destructive instinct. We have even committed the heresy of explaining the origin of human conscience by some such "turning inward" of the aggressive impulse. Obviously when this internal tendency operates on too large a scale, it is no trivial matter; rather, a positively morbid state of things; whereas the diversion of the destructive impulse toward the external world must have beneficial effects. Here is then the biological justification for all those vile, pernicious propensities which we are not combating. We can but own that they are really more akin to nature than this our stand against them, which, in fact, remains to be accounted for.

All this may give you the impression that our theories amount to a species of mythology and a gloomy one at that! But does not every natural science lead ultimately to this—a sort of mythology? Is it otherwise today with your physical sciences?

The upshot of these observations, as bearing on the subject in hand, is that there is no likelihood of our being able to suppress humanity's aggressive tendencies. In some happy corners of the earth, they say, where nature brings forth abundantly whatever man desires, there flourish races whose lives go gently by, unknowing of aggression or constraint. This I can hardly credit; I would like further details about these happy folk. The Bolshevists, too, aspire to do away with human aggressiveness by insuring the satisfaction of material needs and enforcing equality between man and man. To me this hope seems vain. Meanwhile they busily perfect their armaments, and their hatred of outsiders is not the least of the factors of cohesion among themselves. In any case, as you too have observed, complete suppression of man's aggressive tendencies is not in issue; what we may try is to divert it into a channel other than that of warfare.

From our "mythology" of the instincts we may easily deduce a formula for an indirect method of eliminating war. If the propensity for war be due to the destructive instinct, we have always its counteragent, Eros, to our hand. All that produces ties of sentiment between man and man must serve us as war's antidote. These ties are of two kinds. First, such relations as those toward a beloved object, void though they be of sexual intent. The psychoanalyst need feel no compunction in mentioning "love" in this connection; religion uses the same language: Love thy neighbor as thyself. A pious injunction, easy to enounce, but hard to carry out! The other bond of sentiment is by way of identification. All that brings out the significant resemblances between men calls into play this feeling of community, identification, whereon is founded, in large measure, the whole edifice of human society.

In your strictures on the abuse of authority I find another suggestion for an indirect attack on the war impulse. That men are divided into the leaders and the led is but another manifestation of their inborn and irremediable inequality. The second class constitutes the vast majority; they need a high command to make decisions for them, to which decisions they usually bow without demur. In this context we would point out that men should be at greater pains than heretofore to form a superior class of independent thinkers, unamenable to intimidation and fervent in the quest of truth, whose function it would be to guide the masses dependent on their lead. There is no need to point out how little the rule of politicians and the Church's ban on liberty of thought encourage such a new creation. The ideal conditions would obviously be found in a community where every man subordinated his instinctive life to the dictates of reason. Nothing less than this could bring about so thorough and so durable a union between men, even if this involved the severance of mutual ties of sentiment. But surely such a hope is utterly utopian, as things are. The other indirect methods of preventing war are certainly more feasible, but entail no quick results. They conjure up an ugly picture of mills that grind so slowly that, before the flour is ready, men are dead of hunger.

As you see, little good comes of consulting a theoretician, aloof from worldly contact, on practical and urgent problems! Better it were to tackle each successive crisis with means that we have ready to our hands. However, I would like to deal with a question which, though it is not mooted in your letter, interests me greatly. Why do we, you and I and many another, protest so vehemently against war, instead of just accepting it as another of life's odious importunities? For it seems a natural thing enough, biologically sound and practically unavoidable. I trust you will not be shocked by my raising such a question. For the better conduct of an inquiry it may be well to don a mask of feigned aloofness. The answer to my query may run as follows: Because every man has a right over his own life and war destorys lives that were full of promise; it forces the individual into situations that shame his manhood, obliging him to murder fellow men, against his will; it ravages material amenities, the fruits of human toil, and much besides. Moreover, wars, as now conducted, afford no scope for acts of heroism according to the old ideals and, given the high perfection of modern arms, war today would mean the sheer extermination of one of the combatants, if not of both. This is so true, so obvious, that we can but wonder why the conduct of war is not banned by general consent. Doubtless either of the points I have just made is open to debate. It may be asked if the community, in its turn, cannot claim a right over the individual lives of its members. Moreover, all forms of war cannot be indiscriminately condemned; so long as there are nations and empires, each prepared callously to exterminate its rival, all alike must be equipped for war. But we will not dwell on any of these problems; they lie outside the debate to which you have invited me. I pass on to another point, the basis, as it strikes me, of our common hatred of war. It is this: We cannot do otherwise than hate it. Pacifists we are, since our organic nature wills us to be. Hence it comes easy to us to find arguments that justify our standpoint.

This point, however, calls for elucidation. Here is the way in which I see it. The cultural development of mankind (some, I know, prefer to call it civilization) has been in progress since immemorial antiquity. To this *processus* we owe all that is best in our composition, but also much that makes for human suffering. Its origins and causes are obscure, its issue is uncertain, but some of its characteristics are easy to perceive. It well may lead to the extinction of mankind, for it impairs the sexual function in more than one respect, and even today the uncivilized races and the backward classes of all nations are multiplying more rapidly than the cultured elements. This process may, perhaps, be likened to the effects of domestication on certain animals—it clearly involves physical changes of structure—but the view that cultural development is an organic process of this order has not yet become generally familiar. The psychic changes which accompany this process of cultural change are striking, and not to be gainsaid. They consist in the progressive rejection of instinctive ends and a scaling down of instinctive reactions. Sensations which delighted our forefathers have become neutral or unbearable to us; and, if our ethical and aesthetic ideals have undergone a change, the causes of this are ultimately organic. On the psychological side two of the most important phenomena of culture are, firstly, a strengthening of the intellect, which tends to master our instinctive life, and, secondly, an introversion of the aggressive impulse, with all its consequent benefits and perils. Now war runs most emphatically counter to the psychic disposition imposed on us by the growth of culture; we are therefore bound to resent war, to find it utterly intolerable. With pacifists like us it is not merely an intellectual and affective repulsion, but a constitutional intolerance, an idiosyncrasy in its most drastic form. And it would seem that the aesthetic ignominies of warfare play almost as large a part in this repugnance as war's atrocities.

How long have we to wait before the rest of men turn pacifist? Impossible to say, and yet perhaps our hope that these two factors— man's cultural disposition and a well-founded dread of the form that future wars will take—may serve to put an end to war in the near future, is not chimerical. But by what ways or byways this will come about, we cannot guess. Meanwhile we may rest on the assurance that whatever makes for cultural development is working also against war.

With kindest regards and, should this exposé prove a disappointment to you, my sincere regrets,

Yours,

Sigmund Freud

Yale University *New Haven, Connecticut 06510*

SCHOOL OF MEDICINE

June 13, 1967

General Leslie R. Groves
2101 Connecticut Ave., N. W.
Washington, D. C.

Dear General Groves:

I have been working on a comparative biography of Albert Einstein
and Sir Isaac Newton. The project is coming along reasonably well
and may be completed in the near future. I would appreciate very
much getting your opinion on a single point. How much effect do
you believe the letter that Einstein signed, which was drafted by
other physicists, had in shortening the time of development of the
atomic bomb? Do you believe that it had no effect at all? Did it
decrease the time by one-half a year or a year? I realize that the
bomb would have been developed without the letter, but there seems
to be an attempt to indicate that the letter was insignificant. For
example, on page 119 in the recent book by C. P. Snow entitled,
Variety of Men, it is claimed that the Americans were much slower
than the English in this regard. Because you were so close to the
problem and because it is important to have this point in its true
perspective, I would appreciate knowing your views on this subject.

Sincerely yours,

Aaron B. Lerner

Aaron B. Lerner, MD

Dr. Lerner to General Leslie R. Groves

LIEUTENANT GENERAL LESLIE R. GROVES
2101 CONNECTICUT AVENUE, N. W.
WASHINGTON, D. C. 20008

July 12, 1967

Dear Dr. Lerner:

This is in reply to your letter of 13 June, 1967 with its query re Einstein. His letter of October 11, 1939, was written long before I became responsible for atomic development so that I cannot speak too definitely.

I have always understood that Alexander Sachs was the man who concluded that such a letter would be useful to him in his contemplated visit to President Roosevelt, that the letter was drafted by Wigner and Szilard along lines proposed by Sachs, reviewed and revised by Sachs and then taken by Wigner and possibly Szilard to Einstein for signature, after which it was turned over to Sachs for delivery. (Sachs and Wigner are still alive and could give you an accurate account.)

The immediate effect was to strengthen Sachs' presentation to President Roosevelt, the result of which was to initiate government interest in the atomic field. It was over two years from then before the project really got started at all. By November 1941 only 16 laboratory projects totalling some $300,000 had been approved and it was not until June 18, 1942 that the Army Engineers began to play a part in atomic affairs. I believe it is fair to say that full Army responsibility came not long after the time I was placed in charge on Sept 17, 1942.

During the first two years 1939-1941, I am certain that there was a great loss of time. I am sure too that this period would not have even begun when it did if it had not been for the Einstein letter. It took a signature such as his to stir Roosevelt's imagination. I would hestitate to say just how much time was saved— it could have been a few months, it might have been a year. How much time saved in the slow-moving period (1939-1941) would have meant in time saved on the overall project is hard to say. It could have been day for day but I am inclined to think it would have been much less. As a matter of fact I believe that if this period of relative (as compared to Sept 19, 1942 to VJ Day) inactivity had extended much beyond June 1942 it is not at all certain that the Manhattan Project would have been initiated.

I have not seen Snow's "Variety of Men" but I can say that the English were destinctly ahead of the U.S. up to the summer of 1942 in their realization of the importance of developing atomic energy and in certain of their overall studies on the subject. These studies were in the main theoretical supported in some instances by limited laboratory work. This phase is well covered by Margaret Gowing in her book "Britain and Atomic Energy 1939-1945"

I would point out though that the English even if conditions had been normal in Great Britain could never have completed the Project as rapidly as we did.

I doubt if I have answered your question as concisely as you might have hoped but I have tried to give you sufficient background to enable you to reach a conclusion. I hope my reply will be helpful.

Sincerely

Leslie R Groves

I regret that a temporary lack of secretarial assistance has forced me to give you this long hand letter. I hope you can read it easily. LRG

General Groves' reply

214

in the City of New York

NEW YORK, N.Y. 10027

June 27, 1967

Professor Aaron B. Lerner
School of Medicine
Yale University
333 Cedar Street
New Haven, Connecticut

Dear Professor Lerner:

     The period to which you refer is shrouded in mystery to me. I am
inclined to think that Einstein's letter had little effect and that the intervention
of Szilard, Fermi, Wigner, Weisskopf and Teller had little positive influence.
At that time they were hardly the kind of people to move a conservative military
establishment. It is to be regretted that the significant personalities in American
physics, such as Pegram, Millikan, the Compton brothers, as well as the officers
of the National Academy of Science, did not take a greater initiative in this
matter, which really would have had the effect of accelerating the American
effort. This lack of participation is an indication of how wide the gulf was at
that time between science and government.

                                        Sincerely yours,

                                        I. I. Rabi

IIR:it

I. I. Rabi to Dr. Lerner

OAK RIDGE NATIONAL LABORATORY
OPERATED BY
UNION CARBIDE CORPORATION
NUCLEAR DIVISION

POST OFFICE BOX X
OAK RIDGE, TENNESSEE 37830

September 19, 1967

Dr. A. B. Lerner
Yale University
School of Medicine
333 Cedar Street
New Haven, Connecticut

Dear Dr. Lerner:

I am sorry I have not answered your letter of August 18 before now. It is a difficult letter to answer. It is quite possible that the course of events would have been very much the same without the Einstein letter. On the other hand, it is also possible that it was the letter which tipped the balance and thus had a very great impact. If it did, there are probably three or four other factors which were similarly important. The question is really, "Was the decision a close one or was it more or less a foregone conclusion?" My impression is that it was a reasonably close one.

Sincerely yours,

Eugene P. Wigner

EPW:bc

Eugene P. Wigner to Dr. Lerner

Biographical Sketches

John Locke

John Locke, the English physician and philosopher, was born on August 29, 1632, in Wrington, Somerset. On October 28, 1704, he died of congestive heart failure secondary to chronic bronchitis and emphysema in Oates, Essex, a community near London. (Spinoza was also born in 1632.) Locke was educated at Oxford. His medical teachers included the well-known Dr. Thomas Willis of Oxford and Dr. Thomas Sydenham of London. Locke's friendship with Newton began in 1689 and lasted 15 years. At the age of 58, Locke published his great work, *Essay Concerning Human Understanding*.

William Stuckeley

William Stuckeley, Newton's countryman from Lincolnshire and his first biographer, lived from 1688 to 1765. He practiced medicine in London. Shortly before Newton died, Dr. Stuckeley moved to Grantham to begin collecting information on Newton's personal life.

Max Talmey

Max Talmey, born Max Talmud, was born on August 23, 1869, in Tauroggen, Lithuania and died of chronic myocarditis on November 6, 1941, in New York City. Dr. Talmey was a versatile, brilliant student who was graduated *magna cum laude*. He earned money by tutoring part time while in medical school and full time in the summer when he lived with his family in Posen, Poland. His interests included astronomy, music, a universal language, sports, and chess.

Max Talmey and his older brother, Bernard, who preceded him as a weekly guest of the Einstein family, emigrated to America at the turn of the century. Bernard Talmey became a psychiatrist and wrote books and several papers on psychiatry. Max Talmey became an eye, ear, nose, and throat specialist who specialized in surgery of the eye. In 1906 he wrote a textbook for self-instruction in a universal language, in 1910 a psychiatry book for beginners, and in 1932 a book on relativity for laymen. He made a great contribution to medicine in 1916 when he suggested that some cases of poliomyelitis might be related to tonsillectomy, a view not confirmed until the 1940s. In addition he thought that tonsillar tissue played a part in the control of infection, an idea accepted only now.

Moritz Katzenstein

Moritz Katzenstein was born in Rotenburg, Germany, on August 14, 1872, and died in Berlin on March 23, 1932 of uremia secondary to malignant nephrosclerosis. Dr. Katzenstein first met Einstein after performing an abdominal operation on Einstein's stepdaughter, Margot. The two men became good friends and for more than ten years sailed together in one another's boats during the summer. Einstein contrasted his own freedom to study as he pleased with Katzenstein's countless obligations to his patients and to surgical duties. Dr. Katzenstein gave up full-time practice to become chief of surgery at one of the city hospitals. He worked part time at a private clinic and served on the clinical staff of the University of Berlin, first as an instructor and, from 1913 on, as an associate professor. Like Max Talmey, he made an important medical discovery that was recognized only after his death. In 1903 Dr. Katzenstein found that twisting the renal artery of the rabbit caused an increase in blood pressure. It was not until Goldblatt's detailed studies in 1940 that the relationship between blood flow in the renal artery and development of high blood pressure was understood.

Heinrich Zangger

Heinrich Zangger, the only son of farmer parents, was born in

Zurich, Switzerland on December 6, 1874. In his long life he suffered toxic reactions to carbon monoxide, tetraethyl of lead and other chemicals beginning with experiments carried out in high school. During the last several years of his life Dr. Zangger was confined to bed where he continued his work. He died in the city of his birth at the age of 83 on March 15, 1957. In quite different ways, he and Max Talmey had the opportunity to help Einstein more than other physicians did.

The single major trait common to all of Einstein's medical friends was versatility, and Zangger stood at the top of the list. An amazing man with seemingly unlimited interests, he received honorary doctorate degrees in law, philosophy and technical science. Early in college he concentrated on mathematics, physics, and biology. After he received the bachelor's degree, he studied in Italy and also attended lectures by Pierre Curie in Paris. He became keenly interested in colloid chemistry, physiology, pathology, internal medicine and philosophy. He knew many people in the arts, theatre, and science.

In 1902 Zangger returned to Zurich to teach physiology, anatomy, and internal medicine. At the age of 31 in 1905, he became professor of legal medicine and director of the Forensic Medical Institute of Zurich University. He held that position for more than 35 years. He could be counted on as a substitute lecturer in pathology, pharmacology, and neurology. At one time he was dean of the medical school. A world authority and writer on preventive and occupational medicine, he anticipated health problems arising from increased industrialization and gave invaluable help in mine disasters, floods, and major railway accidents. With the spirit of a missionary he used his medical knowledge to help his fellow men.

Hans Mühsam

Hans Mühsam was born in Berlin, Germany on July 15, 1876 and died from the complications of Parkinson's disease in Haifa, Israel on January 31, 1957. He spent his youth in Luebeck where his father was a pharmacist, and he served in the German Army early in the First World War. In 1915 while in general practice in Berlin, he took care of Einstein's ailing mother and met Einstein. Because Dr. Mühsam was interested in mathematics and physical chemistry and had humanitarian goals similar to Einstein's, the two became close friends. Year after year on Sunday afternoons they strolled in the Gruenwald discussing subjects of mutual interest. Mühsam wanted to learn about the relativity theory, and Einstein liked to hear about biology. Together they wrote an article on the pore size of membranes—Einstein's only original report in a medical journal. Dr. Mühsam's niece, Betty Newman, was Einstein's secretary in the early 1920s.

Dr. Mühsam loved medicine and was committed to his patients in Germany. His brother, however, was murdered by the Nazis and by 1938, he had to leave Germany for Israel. Shortly before then symptoms of Parkinson's disease appeared. He also developed glaucoma. As both disorders progressed, Dr. Mühsam became totally incapacitated and blind. Einstein's letters, read to him, provided moments of light.

Rudolf Richard Ehrmann

Rudolf Richard Ehrmann was born on February 3, 1879, in Hessen-Nassau, Germany and died on December 21, 1963, in Berkeley, California from complications following prostatic surgery. Dr. Ehrmann, an internist specializing in gastroenterology, had an excellent background in chemistry. He was Einstein's personal physician as well as a close friend. After their emigration to the United States, they continued their relationship. Dr. Ehrmann served on the staff of the New York University School of Medicine. He visited Einstein during his terminal illness.

Janos Plesch

Janos Plesch was born on November 18, 1878, in Budapest and died suddenly from either a heart attack or stroke on February 28, 1957, in Beverly Hills, California. He suffered recurrent thromboses of the legs for several years, a severe heart attack in 1945, and a mild stroke in 1950.

Dr. Plesch, a brilliant practitioner of internal medicine, wrote extensively on diseases of the blood vessels and heart. Energetic and popular, he knew many people, particularly in the arts and sciences. His knowledge of music, art, and literature was great.

Einstein and Plesch first met in the early 1920s through mutual acquaintances, probably musical friends, and often visited each other. In his autobiography, written in 1949, Dr. Plesch discussed famous people he knew, including Einstein.

Rudolf Nissen

Rudolf Nissen was born in Neisse, Germany on September 9, 1896. His father was a surgeon. Young Nissen studied medicine at the universities of Munich, Marburg, and Breslau. From 18 to 22 he served in the German Army. Two of these years were spent as a battalion surgeon, and he was wounded twice. To provide a broad basis for a career in surgery, he trained in medicine and pathology. He studied with Oscar Minkowski, a pioneer in the cause of diabetes and a relative of the mathematician, Hermann Minkowski. In pathology he worked with Ludwig Aschoff. Dr. Nissen held academic positions at the universities of Munich and Berlin and was associated with Ferdinand Sauerbruch in Berlin. After Hitler came to power, Nissen, whose mother had been Jewish, left Germany. He became head of the department of surgery at the University of Istanbul in 1933 and stayed there till 1939. He spent a year at the Massachusetts General Hospital and in 1941 was made chief of surgery at the Brooklyn Jewish Hospital, a post he held for 11 years. From 1944 to 1950 he was chief surgeon at Maimonides Hospital in Brooklyn. In 1952 Dr. Nissen returned to Europe to become head of the department of surgery at the University of Basel in Switzerland where he now lives. He has been an accomplished surgeon and has authored some 500 works, including books and papers pertaining to thoracic and abdominal surgery.

Dr. Nissen first met Einstein in Berlin in the early 1930s at the home of a mutual physician friend, probably Katzenstein. In December 1947, he operated on Einstein at the Brooklyn Jewish Hospital and found a large aneurysm of the abdominal aorta. A few years later Einstein, harassed by photographers, was photographed with his tongue sticking out at them. He got a copy of the picture and sent it to Nissen with the comment: "To Nissen my tummy/the world my tongue."

Gustav Bucky

Gustav Bucky was born on September 3, 1880, in Leipzig, Germany and died of a melanoma on February 19, 1963, in New York City. The friendship between Bucky and Einstein increased after both came to the United States. Dr. Bucky invented the Bucky Diaphragm for X-ray machines and was one of the first to use Grenz ray therapy. Together with Einstein he invented an automatic exposure device for X-rays.

Otto Juliusburger

Otto Juliusburger was born in Breslau, Germany, on September 26, 1867, and died in New York City of cardiac failure on June 7, 1952. Dr. Juliusburger was a well-known psychiatrist in Berlin and a founder of one of the first psychoanalytical societies in that city. He and Einstein shared many sentiments about the problems of mankind.

Gabriel Segall

Gabriel Segall was born on March 8, 1895, in Libau, Latvia, and died of myocardial infarction at age 68 in Los Angeles on December 10, 1963. After completing elementary and secondary schooling in Germany, he studied medicine at the University of Berlin. He emigrated to the United States in 1922 and, a few months later, began practicing internal medicine in Los Angeles. Dr. Segall had broad interests in medicine and the humanities. Einstein and Segall first met in January 1931 in Pasadena. They held similar humanitarian attitudes and maintained a lively correspondence. The two men saw each other again in Princeton in 1949 when Dr. Segall made a trip to the East.

References

Newton

Books

Anthony, H. D. 1961. *Sir Isaac Newton*. New York: Collier Books.

Braybrooke, R. and Smith J., eds. 1855. *Diary and correspondence of Samuel Pepys*. Vol. IV. Philadelphia: J.B. Lippincott and Co.

Brewster, D. 1852. *The life of Sir Isaac Newton*. New York: Harper and Brothers.

Brodetsky, S. 1927. *Sir Isaac Newton*. London: Methuen and Co. Ltd.

Cambridge University. 1942. *Newton tercentenary celebrations*. London: Cambridge University Press.

———. 1946. *Newton tercentenary celebrations*. London: Cambridge University Press.

Cohen, I. B. 1956. *Franklin and Newton*. Philadelphia: The American Philosophical Society.

Craig, J. 1946. *Newton at the mint*. London: Cambridge University Press.

de Villamil, R. 1936. *Newton*: *the man*. London: Gordon D. Knox.

Einstein wrote a forward to this book.

Dewhurst, K. 1963. *John Locke*: *physician and philosopher*. London: The Wellcome Historical Medical Library.

Einstein, A. 1960. *Isaac Newton*. In *A chapter in the Smithsonian treasury of Science*. Edited by Webster B. True. Vol. I. New York: Simon and Schuster.

Fontanelle, M. 1728. *The elogium of Sir Isaac Newton*. London: J. Tonson in the Strand.

Hall, A. R. and M. B., eds. 1962. *Unpublished papers of Isaac Newton*. London: Cambridge University Press.

History of Science Society. 1928. *Sir Isaac Newton: a bicentenary evaluation of his work*. Baltimore: The Williams and Wilkins Co.

Hoskin, M. A. and Whiteside, D. T., eds. 1967, 1968. *The mathematical papers of Isaac Newton*. Vols. I and II. London: Cambridge University Press.

King, E. F. 1858. *Biographical sketch of Sir Isaac Newton*. Grantham: S. Ridge and Son; London: Simpkin, Marshall and Co.

McLachlan, H. 1950. *Isaac Newton: theological manuscripts*. Liverpool: University Press.

Manuel, F. E. 1963. *Isaac Newton: historian*. Cambridge, Mass.: Belknap Press (Harvard University).

———. 1968. *A portrait of Isaac Newton*. Cambridge, Mass.: Belknap Press (Harvard University).

More, L. T. 1934. *Isaac Newton: a biography*. New York: Charles Scribner's Sons.

North, J. D. 1967. *Isaac Newton*. London: Oxford University Press.

Rigaud, S. P. 1738. *Historical essay concerning the first publication of Sir Isaac Newton's Principia*. London: Oxford University Press.

Scott, J. F. 1967. *The correspondence of Isaac Newton*. Vol. IV. London: Cambridge University Press.

Shirras, G. F. 1950. *Newton: a study of a master mind*. Amsterdam: *Tirage à Part des Actes du V Congres D'Histoire des Sciences*.

Stukeley, W. 1936. *Memoirs of Sir Isaac Newton's life*. London: Taylor and Francis.

Sullivan, J. W. N. 1938. *Isaac Newton*. New York: The Macmillan Co.

Turnbull, H. W. 1945. *Mathematical discoveries of Newton*. London: Blackie and Son, Ltd.

――. ed. 1959, 1960, 1961. *The correspondence of Isaac Newton*. Vols. I, II, III. London: Cambridge University Press.

Withington, E. T. 1909. *John Locke as a medical practitioner*. Holland: Harlem.

Articles

British Astronomical Association. November 1956. Edmund Halley: papers to commemorate the tercentenary of his birth. *Memoirs of the British Astronomical Association*. Vol. 37.

Brody, J. E. February 18, 1968. It can be tough to be first born. *New York Times*: E-8.

Brown, P. L. 1967. The Isaac Newton telescope. *New Scientist* 36: 536-539.

McKie, D. 1942. Newton and chemistry. *Endeavor* 1: 141 ff.

Reinhold, R. September 23, 1971. Isaac Newton revival. *New York Times*: 37.

Book Reviews

Eisele, C. 1967. *The mathematical papers of Isaac Newton*. Vol. I. *Science* 158: 245-6.

Hartley, H. 1962. *The correspondence of Isaac Newton*. Vol. III. *New Scientist*. 13: 222.

――. 1967. *The correspondence of Isaac Newton*. Vol. IV. *New Scientist* 35: 449.

――. 1967. *The mathematical papers of Isaac Newton*. Vol. I. *New Scientist* 34: 360.

Osman, T. 1967. *Isaac Newton*. J. D. North. *Newton and gravitation*. Colin Brooks. *New Scientist*. 36: 621.

Price, D. J. D. 1967. *The correspondence of Isaac Newton*. Vol. IV. *Science* 158: 1298.

Wheeler, F. 1968. *Letters on wave mechanics*. *New Scientist* 38: 251-2.

Einstein

Books

Barnett, L. 1948. *The universe and Dr. Einstein*. New York: William Sloane Associates.

Bergmann, P. G. 1968. *The riddle of gravitation*. New York: Charles Scribner's Sons.

Bernstein, J. 1967. *A comprehensible world*. New York: Random House.

Born, I., trans. 1971. *The Born-Einstein letters: correspondence between Albert Einstein and Max and Hedwig Born, 1920-1955*. New York: Walker and Company.

Einstein, A. 1934. *Essays in science*. New York: Philosophical Library.

———. 1950. *Out of my later years*. New York: Philosophical Library.

———. 1956. *Investigations on the theory of Brownian movement*. Edited by Ruth A. Furth. Translated by A. D. Cowper. New York: Dover Publications, Inc.

Frank. P. 1963. *Einstein: his life and times*. Translated by George Rosen. New York: Alfred A. Knopf.

Philipp Frank's book gives the best report on Einstein's life in Prague.

Hoffmann, B. and Dukas, H. 1972. *Albert Einstein: Creator and Rebel*. New York: Viking.

Infeld, L. 1950. *Albert Einstein: his work and its influence on our world*. New York: Charles Scribner's Sons.

———. 1941. *Quest: The evolution of a scientist*. New York: Charles Scribner's Sons.

Klein, M. J. 1970. *Paul Ehrenfest*. New York: American Elsevier Publishing Company, Inc.

Lanczos, C. 1965. *Albert Einstein and the cosmic world order*. New York: Interscience Publishers.

Moore, R. 1967. *Niels Bohr: the man and the scientist*. London: Hodder and Stoughton.

Moszkowski, A. 1921. *Einstein: einblicke in seine Gedankenwelt* Hamburg: Hoffmannn and Campe.

Nathan O. and Norden H., eds. 1960. *Einstein on peace*. New York: Simon and Schuster.

An excellent book that gives a clear picture of Einstein's personality.

Plesch, J. 1949. *Janos: the story of a doctor*. Translated by Edward Fitzgerald. London: Victor Gollanez, Ltd.

Przibram, K., ed. 1967. *Letters on wave mechanics*. Translated by M. J. Klein. London: Vision Press.

Schilpp, P. A. 1949. *Albert Einstein: philosopher-scientist*. New York: Tudor Publishing Co.

This book contains the only autobiography written by Einstein as well as a complete bibliography up to 1949.

Seelig, C. 1956. *Albert Einstein: a documentary biography*. Translated by Mervyn Savill. London: Staples Press Limited.

——. 1956. *Helle zeit, dunkle zeit: in memoriam, Albert Einstein*. Zurich: Europa Verlag.

Carl Seelig described Einstein's life in Switzerland better than anyone else.

Snow, C. P. 1967. *Variety of men*. New York: Charles Scribner's Sons.

Talmey, M. 1932. *The relativity theory simplified*. New York: Falcon Press.

Articles

Baker, S. S. April 6, 1972. Einstein the poet. *New York Times: Letters to the Editor*.

Bergmann, P. G. 1956. Fifty years of relativity. *Science* 123: 487 ff.

Bernstein, J. April 16, 1966. Einstein and Bohr: a debate. *The New Yorker*: 174 ff.

Blank, J. P. and Bucky, T. L. September 1964. Einstein: an intimate memoir. *Harper's*: 43 ff.

Burt, C. 1965. Child prodigies. *New Scientist* 28: 122 ff.

Christies of London Catalogue. November 29, 1967. Important autograph letters, manuscripts, and printed books. 62-66

Holton, G. 1971-72. On trying to understand scientific genius. *American Scholar* 41: 95 ff.

——. 1967-68. Influence of Einstein's early work in relativity theory. *American Scholar* 37: 59-79.

Infeld, L. February 1965. As I see it. *Bulletin of the Atomic Scientists*: 7 ff.

Kapitza, P. L. 1966. Recollections of Lord Rutherford. *Nature* 210: 780 ff.

Kilmister, C. W. 1963. Gravitation after Einstein. *New Scientist* 19: 34 ff.

Klein, M. J. January 1965. Einstein and some civilized discontents. *Physics Today*: 38 ff.

——. 1967. Thermodynamics in Einstein's thought. *Science* 157: 509-516.

Lang, D. July 25, 1965. The writer and the scientist. *New York Times Book Review*: 6.

Lapp, R. E. August 2, 1964. The Einstein letter that started it all. *New York Times Magazine*: 13 ff.

McCrea, W. H. 1955. Obituary—Albert Einstein. *Nature* 175: 925.

——. 1966. Einstein's greatest contribution. *New Scientist* 29: 716 ff.

New York Times. December 22, 1971. Obituary—Mrs. Frances Nash Watson.

Pulse—The Magazine of the Albert Einstein College of Medicine. Spring 1959. Memorial issue.

Smith, R. A. 1962. Masers and lasers. *Endeavor* 21: 108 ff.

Stubbs, P. 1967. General relativity in the dock. *New Scientist* 33: 326 ff.

Sullivan, W. March 27, 28, 29, 1972. The Einstein Papers. *New York Times*.

Talmey, Max. October 3 and October 10, 1924. Albert Einstein. *The Sentinel: The American Jewish Weekly*.

Whitrow, G. J., ed. 1967. Einstein: the man and his achievement. British Broadcasting Company Third Program Talks.

Book Reviews

Holton, G. September 5, 1971. *Einstein: the life and times*. Ronald Clark. *New York Times Book Review*: 1.

Klein, M. J. 1968. *Erwin Schrödinger: an introduction to his writings*. William J. Scott. *Science* 159: 967-8.

———. 1970a. *My life and views*. Max Born. *Science* 169: 360-1.

———. 1970b. *Briefwechsel 1916-1955: Albert Einstein and Hedwig and Max Born*. Edited by Max Born. *Science* 169: 360-1.

———. 1970c. *Physics in my generation*. Max Born. *Science* 169: 360-1.

———. 1971. *Einstein: the life and times*. Ronald Clark. *Science*. 174: 1315-16.

Index

AARON B. LERNER was born in Minneapolis in 1920 and was educated in the public schools there and at the University of Minnesota, where he received his BA, PhD, and MD degrees. He has held research or teaching positions at the Army Chemical Center and at the medical schools of Case Western Reserve University, the University of Michigan, and the University of Oregon. Since 1955 Dr. Lerner has been at Yale University where he is professor of dermatology and chairman of the Department of Dermatology. His major research interests, beginning when he was an undergraduate, have been in the biochemistry of normal and malignant pigment cells. His numerous contributions to the field of pigment cell biology are well known. He is a member of the National Academy of Sciences.

Dr. Lerner's curiosity about what makes an individual successful, coupled with his long-standing interest in the physical and biological sciences, led him to study and compare the lives and achievements of Einstein and Newton.